INTERSPECIES
STORY: Amahara
ART: masha

CONTENTS
CHAPTER 36 ...... P003
CHAPTER 37 ...... P021
CHAPTER 38 ...... P043
CHAPTER 39 ...... P061
CHAPTER 40 ...... P077
CHAPTER 41 ...... P093
CHAPTER 42 ...... P111
BONUS P125

STUNK! ZEL!
THERE'S SOMEONE BY THE ENTRANCE WHO SAYS SHE NEEDS TO TALK TO YOU OR SOMETHING!
GAYA (CHATTER)
GAYA
HUH?
WHO'S HERE FOR US?
GACHA (GACHIK)
HEEEEEY! ♥
GYO (HURK)
HEY THERE!
BEEN A WHILE!
THERE'S SOMETHING I WANTED TO TALK TO YOU ABOUT. DO YOU HAVE A SECOND?
ZORO (CROWD)
ZORO

CHAPTER 36
ゴポ
GOPO
ゴポ
GOPO (BLURK)
SALAMANDER
FIRE DRAGON'S
FEM-FLESH BBQ
ゴポ
GOPO

WOW, I CAN'T BELIEVE IT.
A HUMAN AND AN ELF MAKING A RETURN VISIT?
BOU (BWOOF)
MERA (FWOOM)
PACHI (KRAKKL)
PACHI
YOU'RE MY FIRST CUSTOMERS TO EVER DO THAT!
BO (BFF)
BO
WELL, Y'KNOW.
JUUUUUU (SIZZZZLE)
PACHI
SALAMANDER BARBECUE IS JUST PLAIN TASTY TOO.
MERA

SEEMS YOU EVEN CAME NICE AND PREPARED FOR THE HEAT.
JUWAAA (SIZZZZZ)
DOES THAT MEAN I CAN EXPECT SOME OF YOUR MEAT THIS TIME AS WELL?
NATU-RALLY!
THAT'S WHY WE'RE HERE!

REWINDING TO YESTERDAY...
KORO (RATTLE)
KORON
WHAT'RE THESE?
LOOKS LIKE MAGIC RINGS OR SOMETHING.
YOU SEE, THOSE...

DON (BOOM)
...ARE (PROTOTYPE) FULL FIRE RESISTANCE RINGS I MADE...
...BY RESEARCHING YOUR ANGEL FRIEND'S RESISTANCES!

I'D LIKE THEM TO EVENTUALLY GIVE RESISTANCE TO EVERYTHING...
...BUT FIRE IS THE MOST I CAN MANAGE AT THE MOMENT.
FIRE
RESIST!
THAT'S WHERE MY REQUEST FOR YOU COMES IN—
I WANT YOU TO WEAR THOSE RINGS...
BISHI (POINT)

...SPEND SOME TIME IN BED WITH A SALAMANDER, AND WRITE A REVIEW OF IT!
YOUR REWARD WILL BE 200,000G!!
WOOOW! ♥
HUH!?
WHY!?
WAIT, HOLD ON.
HOW DO YOU STAND TO GAIN ANYTHING HERE?
CAN'T YOU USE OTHER ADVENTURERS IF YOU JUST WANT TO TEST RESISTANCE?
AND FOR CHEAPER...
THIS SEEMS A LITTLE TOO GOOD TO BE TRUE.
OH, I GET PLENTY OUT OF IT! ♪
JUST THINK!

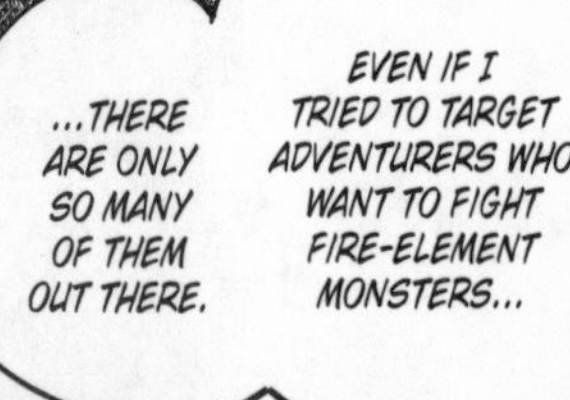
EVEN IF I TRIED TO TARGET ADVENTURERS WHO WANT TO FIGHT FIRE-ELEMENT MONSTERS...
...THERE ARE ONLY SO MANY OF THEM OUT THERE.

BUT...
...HOW MANY MEN WANT TO HAVE FUN WITH A SALAMANDER?
HUNDREDS OF THOUSANDS, RIGHT?

OH...!
TRUE!

AND YOU KNOW, YOUR REVIEWS...
...HAVE A GOOD BIT OF INFLUENCE.

IF YOU GUYS WROTE A SALAMANDER REVIEW...
BAAAN (BAAAM)
...THAT'D BE AMAZING PUBLICITY FOR THIS PRODUCT!

I... I GUESS YOU REALLY MIGHT BE ABLE TO SELL A TON OF THEM...!

THE ONLY WAY TO DO IT WITH A SALAMANDER RIGHT NOW IS TO MARRY HER AND TO BE ON THE RECEIVING END OF A MIRACLE FROM GOD...

WHOA...

OH, AND BRING YOUR ANGEL BUDDY ALONG WITH YOU.

I WANT TO COMPARE THE RINGS TO SOMEONE WITH THE SAME RESISTANCE LEVEL.

HM? WELL, FINE WITH US.

THE READERS LIKE IT BETTER WHEN HE COMES ALONG ANYWAY.

OKAY! THEN IT'S TIME TO GO TO THE VOLCANIC LANDS!

HUH?

YOU'RE COMING TOO, MISS DEMIA?

I'LL HEAL YOU UP IF YOU GET BURNED.

BI (BTT)

...WHICH BRINGS US TO THE PRESENT.
MY BREAST MEAT IS READY TO GO!
JUWAWA (SIZZZZLE)
TOUCHING'S OKAY HERE, AND IT WON'T BE HOT FOR ME...
...SO I GUESS I'LL GO FOR IT BARE-HANDED...!
AHH! ♥
MUNYU (SQUISH)
HM.
SO?
NOT HOT? EVERYTHING OKAY?
IT'S STILL A LITTLE HOT...
...BUT IT FEELS LIKE IT'S AROUND THE LEVEL OF A HOT BATH...
IF ANYTHING, THIS MIGHT ACTUALLY BE NICE AND WARM.
MUGU MUGU (MUNCH)
MERA MERA MERA (FWOOM)
STUNK! YOU'RE ON FIRE! YOUR CLOTHES!!

AAAGH!
MY CAPE!
SU (SST)
ALL THE OXYGEN AROUND HIS CAPE—
AWAY!!
WHOA!
BO (BWOOF)
HA-HA-HA! SORRY ABOUT THAT.
HYUOO (WHOOSH)
FORGOT TO WARN YOU THAT IT DOESN'T MAKE YOUR CLOTHES RESISTANT.
I THINK IT'D BE BETTER IF YOU TOOK YOUR SHIRTS OFF.
WHAT KIND OF LOOK WOULD THAT BE...?
AH... UM...
MUGYU (SQUISH)
MISS WITCH?
MUGYU

WHY DO YOU KEEP MAKING ME COOK THE SAME CUT...?
NGH!
BIKU (TWITCH)
GORI (GRIND)
ZUPUN (SPLURCH)
WELL...!
IT'S BECAUSE I WANT TO FIGURE OUT WHICH PART OF YOU MAKES FOR THE MOST MANA-RICH AND TASTY PIECE OF MEAT.
TIME FOR MORE!
!
PUNI (PLURP)
ALL RIGHT, TIME FOR TWO MORE...
...RIGHT IN YOUR MAIN DISH!

NNNNNNNGH!?
HRNNNNNGH!!
ZUPUPU (ZPLUURCH)
AH! AH! AH!
AH HA HA!
CAN'T TAKE MUCH MORE, LITTLE ANGEL?
JUUU (SIZZLE)
GYU (SCRUNCH)
THEN HURRY UP AND FINISH YOUR MEAL SO WE CAN GET A PRIVATE ROOM!

AAHH!
ZUZU
ズズ…

ZU (ZZT)
ズ…

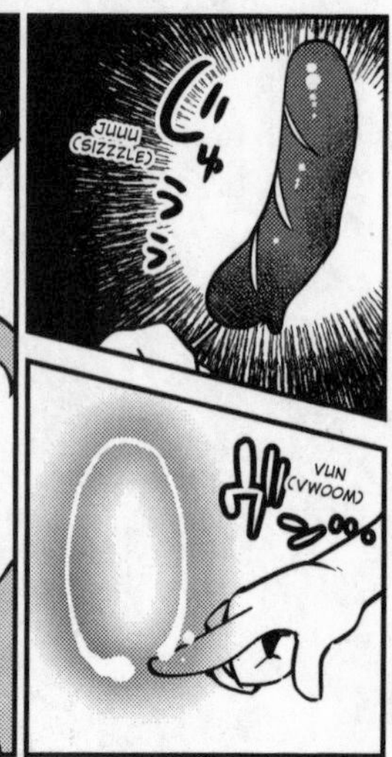
JUUU (SIZZZLE)
じゅううう
VUN (VWOOM)

……
MOGU (MUNCH)
もぐ
MOGU
もぐ
HMM.
MOGU
もぐ

?
WHAT'RE YOU EATING, DEMIA?

YOU REALLY CAN TASTE MORE MANA THAN WHEN YOU COOK THEM OVER MAGIC GEMS...
I WONDER IF I COULD FIGURE OUT A GOOD WAY TO TURN THIS INTO A PRODUCT...
PERO (CLICK)

GIMME SOME!
I'M GETTING HUNGRY FROM ALL THIS RESEARCH WE'VE BEEN DOING.
ZURI ズリ
ズリ ZURI (SLIDE)
SO TINY...
チビ… CHIBI (NIBBLE)
!
パアアアッ PAAA (SHIIINE)

WHAT IS THIS!? IT'S DE-LICIOUS!
HOW DOES IT HAVE SUCH AN INTENSE FIRE MAGIC FLAVOR!?
WHOOA!
THESE TWO IN PARTICULAR! THE TASTE IS EVEN STRONGER AND MORE CONCENTRATED!
HOW DID YOU COOK THESE THINGS!?

STUCK 'EM IN A SALA-MANDER'S ASS AND %+«$@, AND—
BFFFT!

I'M GONNA MURDER YOU!!
GIRI
GIRI
DEMIAAA! YOU...!!
GIRI (GRIND)
GIRI
BARRIER!
YOU'RE GONNA MAKE ME STOP RESEARCHING MY RESISTANCE RING!
OH NOOO, SO SCARY!
PTOO!
YOU CAN LEAVE PRODUCTION AND DISTRI-BUTION TO ME.
YEAH. EVERYTHING IS READY.
MORE IMPORTANTLY, DEATHABYSS!
GRRR...
ARE WE ALL READY TO MASS-PRODUCE AND SELL THESE RINGS?
HOW'S YOUR TEST OF THE PROTO-TYPE, THOUGH?
THAT PART IS YOUR JOB, RIGHT!?

ONE OF MY DECOYS IS WITH THOSE SEX REVIEWERS RIGHT NOW.
THINGS ARE GETTING HOT AND HEAVY WITH A SALAMAN-DER AS WE SPEAK.
EXCUSE ME!?
A PRACTICAL TEST...
...A DETAILED END-USER REPORT...
...AND NATIONAL PUBLICITY FOR THE PRODUCT!
DON'T YOU THINK IT'S A GREAT WAY TO GET ALL THREE DONE AT ONCE?
W-WELL...
PERHAPS YOU'RE RIGHT...

SO?
HOW DID THESE ALL-IMPORTANT RESULTS TURN OUT?
WILL WE BE ABLE TO EARN FUTURE RESEARCH AND CAMPAIGN FUNDS?
LIKE I SAID, THEY'RE RIGHT IN THE MIDDLE OF IT.
I'LL PUT THE ARTICLE UP HERE ONCE IT'S DONE, OKAY?

YORUNO GLOSS REVIEW

ONE SMALL STEP FOR FIRE-ELEMENT MAN...

ONE GIANT SKEET FOR NEUTRAL-ELEMENT MANKIND

TODAY WE'RE HERE TO TALK ABOUT A NEW PRODUCT FROM THAT SEXY DECOY WITCH. WE EQUIPPED ONE OF HER FIRE RESISTANCE RINGS AND WENT TO DO IT WITH A SALAMANDER GIRL. WE STARTED BY GETTING OUR FILL OF MEAT GRILLED RIGHT ON HER BODY. WHAT CAN I SAY, IT WAS SEXY AND TASTY. AFTER THE MEAL, THE TIME HAD COME AND WE MOVED TO A PRIVATE ROOM. IT WAS ABOUT AS HOT AS A HOT BATH, SO WHILE IT FELT NICE, IT WAS A LITTLE SCARY ONCE I WAS IN HER YOU-KNOW-WHERE. I WAS OKAY PUTTING IT IN, BUT AFTER I STARTED MOVING, IT GOT CRAZY HOT. I WAS ABLE TO JUST BARELY FINISH THE DEED, BUT...I WAS SINGED ENOUGH FOR IT TO TINGLE. STILL, HUMANITY HAS AT LAST (SEXUALLY) CONQUERED THE SALAMANDER! A TOAST TO THIS GIANT STEP FORWARD. SHE WAS A PERFECTLY SEXY AND CUTE GIRL OTHERWISE, SO I'D GIVE HER AN EIGHT IF NOT FOR THE HEAT.

THE BODY BARBECUE HERE TASTES SO GOOD THANKS TO THE MANA-SOAKED FLAVOR. I'D RECOMMEND THIS STORE ON THAT ALONE, EVEN WITHOUT THE SEXY STUFF. I HIGHLY SUGGEST THAT YOU CHECK IT OUT. THE PROBLEM, THOUGH, WAS THE SEX. SHE FELT AMAZING IN MY ARMS THANKS TO HER POWERFUL FIRE MANA, BUT...IT WAS TOO HOT INSIDE HER. I THOUGHT THAT MAYBE I'D BE OKAY FOR THE FIRST FEW SECONDS, BUT ONCE I GOT MOVING, I REALIZED...IT WASN'T HAPPENING. STILL, HER MANA-FILLED PHYSIQUE WAS AMAZING, SO I'D WANT TO GIVE THE STORE A NINE IF THE FIRE RESISTANCE RING WAS A LITTLE MORE EFFECTIVE. OF COURSE, IT'S ALREADY RIDICULOUSLY EFFECTIVE WHEN YOU CONSIDER THAT A SHIELD THAT CUTS FIRE DAMAGE IN HALF COSTS NEARLY 100,000G...

THIS WAS MY SECOND TIME WITH A SALAMANDER, SINCE I'M NATURALLY OKAY WITH FIRE. THE BARBECUE WAS DELICIOUS AND HAD A STRONGER MANA FLAVOR THAN ANY MEAT I'D HAD BEFORE. I ALSO LIKED THE POWERFUL SENSE OF PURE FIRE MANA I FELT AS WE FOOLED AROUND, AND AS SOMEONE WHO'S MORE PASSIVE IN BED, I WAS ABLE TO RELAX AND ENJOY IT THANKS TO HER AGGRESSIVE NATURE. BUT IS THERE NO WAY TO ADDRESS THE SMELL AFTER GOING FROM THE GRILL TO THE BEDROOM...? STUNK AND ZEL WENT WITH GIRLS OTHER THAN THE ONE WE COOKED ON, SO THEY WERE ALSO ABLE TO AVOID GETTING SLATHERED IN BARBECUE DRIPPINGS...NOT THAT I CAN COMPLAIN, SINCE WE'D HAVE TO WAIT FOR WAY TOO LONG IF WE ALL PICKED THE SAME GIRL, BUT...I'M JUST LEFT A LITTLE DISSATISFIED.

IT SEEMS THAT THE MANA CONCENTRATION OF THE BARBECUE HERE GOES IN ORDER OF YOU-KNOW-WHERE, ASS, TAIL, MOUTH, AND THE REST OF HER BODY IN ORDER FROM MOST TO LEAST. IF YOU'VE GOT A PROBLEM WITH COOKING INSIDE OF HER, I'D RECOMMEND HER TAIL. I DO THINK IT'S A LITTLE BORING, SINCE IT DOESN'T LOOK THAT NAUGHTY, THOUGH.

I USED SOME DIRTY MAGIC TO GROW A DICK AND TAKE HER TO BED WITH ME, BUT...HAVE YOU EVER TAKEN A CAN OF TEA THAT FEELS WARM IN YOUR HAND AND SHAKEN IT? IT GETS TOO HOT TO EVEN HOLD, RIGHT? I WONDER IF IT'S THE SAME PROBLEM WITH YOUR DICK HERE. IT'S NICE AND WARM IF YOU DON'T START PUMPING AWAY, THOUGH...I'LL BE SURE TO IMPROVE THE FIRE RESISTANCE RINGS TO THE POINT WHERE YOU CAN SAFELY DO THAT BY THE TIME THEY GO ON SALE TO THE PUBLIC, OKAY? WE'RE SHOOTING FOR THE PRICE TO BE 40,000G AT THE MOMENT, BUT IF IT GOES UP AFTER THE IMPROVEMENTS, THEN SORRY!

PURCHASES AND PREORDERS FOR RESISTANCE RINGS SCHEDULED TO BE AVAILABLE AT ALL DEMON KING-OPERATED MAGICAL ARTIFACT DISTRIBUTION CENTERS.

【CONTACT US】 MAGICAL ARTIFACT DISTRIBUTION CENTER — ...

MAGICAL ARTIFACT DISTRIBUTION CENTER — BRANCH ...

...LOOKS LIKE WE'LL NEED A FEW MORE IMPROVEMENTS...

HEY! ARE WE GOING TO BE ALL RIGHT!? HEY!!

HEEEY!

YOU REALIZE WE'VE PUT DOWN AN IMMENSE AMOUNT OF MONEY ON THIS PRODUCTION LINE, RIGHT!?

I GUESS THE RELEASE DATE MIGHT GET DELAYED BY A COUPLE OF WEEKS.

O-OH! SO IS THAT ALL!?

THANK GOODNESS...

OH WELL.

IF YOU ADD CONTACT INFORMATION FOR THESE RINGS AT THE BOTTOM OF YOUR REVIEW, I'LL GIVE YOU ALL FREE THREE-DAY DECOY RENTALS!
SERIOUSLY!?
WE'LL DO IT!
HER BOOBS ARE TOUCHING HIM...HOW LUCKY.
ONE FOR EACH OF US!?

WE'RE FINALLY DONE WITH THAT JOB!
BAN (BOOM)
YOU AROUND, STUNK?
C'MON, LET'S GO AND REVIEW!
HM?
HEY, BROOZ. HEY, KANCHAL.
SORRY, BUT WE'RE GOOD ON GIRLS FOR THE NEXT THREE DAYS OR SO.

CHAPTER 37

UGH! IT'S NO FAIR!
NOT JUST A FIRE RESISTANCE RING TEST...
...BUT THEY GET TO RENT MISS DEMIA TOO!?
I CAN'T BELIEVE YOU GOT AN OFFER THAT SWEET WHILE I WAS AWAY!

ANYWAY! MISS DEMIA!
I'D LIKE ANOTHER THREE DAYS WITH A DECOY!
HEH!
SORRY, BUT NO.
WHY!?
JUST GIVE IT UP, KANCHAL...
WE GOT DOWN ON OUR KNEES AND BEGGED, BUT SHE STILL SAID NO...
GRRRR...

AH-HA-HA, SORRY!
MY REAL BODY IS IN THE DEMON KING'S CASTLE NEARBY, SO I COULD CALL ONE OVER...
...BUT ALL MY OTHER DECOYS ARE BUSY RESEARCHING AND MANUFACTURING FIRE RESISTANCE RINGS RIGHT NOW, SO YOU'RE OUT OF LUCK.
NO WAY...

CALM DOWN... THIS PLACE ISN'T UNDER CHURCH CONTROL ANYWAY.
IT'S AGAINST THE LAW TO CONDUCT ANY SUCCUBUS ACTIVITIES OUTSIDE OF A SUCCUBUS JOINT.

OH... YOU DIDN'T KNOW, BROOZ?
MISS DEMIA IS THE ONE PERSON THAT DOESN'T APPLY TO...
EXACTLY!

HEH...
SUCCU-GIRL ACTIVITIES OUTSIDE OF A STORE...
...ARE NORMALLY A CRIME. HOWEVER...
...DEMIA MAGICAL TOOLS ISN'T REGISTERED AS A SUCCUBUS JOINT, BUT RATHER AS A STORE FOR NAUGHTY MAGICAL GOODS...
...SO IT'S NOT A PROBLEM AT ALL!!
ESSENTIALLY, ALL I'M DOING IS SELLING SUPER-DUPER-ULTRA-HIGH-QUALITY MAGICAL HOLES!
DON (BOOM)
HEH-HEH!
THE SAME GOES FOR THE SUCCUBUS TAX PLACED ON SUCCUBUS JOINTS TOO!
I DON'T PAY A CENT OF IT!
IS THAT SOMETHING TO BE PROUD OF!?

I REALLY DON'T CARE EITHER WAY, BUT...
HAAH...
...JUST DON'T USE YE PUBBE'S LODGING FACILITIES...
...WHILE YOU'VE GOT THOSE DIRTY LADIES AROUND YOU, OKAY?
GINURO (GLARE)
WE'RE NOT A COUPLES' INN HERE, UNDERSTAND?
CRIM?
THAT INCLUDES YOU, OKAY...?
GIRAN (GLINT)
Y-YEAH...
WHAT'S GOT HER ON EDGE?
OH...
?

MAYBE IT'S BECAUSE THIS MORNING, SHE SAW ME...
...TAKING A LOAD OFF HER LITTLE ANGEL?
AH!
AH!
AH!
CRIIIM! IT'S ABOUT TIME FOR YOU TO COME DOWNSTA—
AHAH!
AH!
GACHA (GACHIK)
GISHI (GSSHT)
!
GISHI

OH MY.
WANNA JOIN IN?
ABSOLUTELY NOT!
BAN (SLAM)
DO A GOOD JOB DOWN THERE TODAY! ♥
OKAY...
IF ONLY SHE'D JOINED US THERE, INSTEAD IT'D BE...
..."I CAN'T WAIT FOR ROUND TWO TONIGHT! ♥
"JUST WAIT UNTIL WORK IS OVER, OKAY? HEH-HEH-HEH... ♥"
...YOU KNOW...?
IT'D BE A NICE AND NAUGHTY WORLD WHERE EVERYONE CAME OUT AHEAD.
MHM. MHM.
WE COULD HAVE HAD A PEACEFUL FUTURE! ♥
IRA (IRK)
IRA
...SO WHERE'S CRIM'S DECOY RIGHT NOW—?
...OH, HER?

SHE'S CLEANING UP THE ROOM RIGHT NOW—
FOUND ONE! ♥
AH...AN ANGEL'S HAIR...
HOOOH...
I'M GETTING A HAUL OF RARE MATERIALS JUST BY TIDYING UP...

THIS ROOM'S ALMOST LIKE A MOUNTAIN OF TREASURE... ♥
KIRA
KIRA (SHINE)
キラ
キラ
MAYBE I SHOULD JUST SUGGEST A HAIRCUT.
SEE? ISN'T IT NICE TO HAVE IT SHORT ENOUGH TO NOT SIT ON YOUR WINGS? ♡
きり
DOSSARI (THWOMP)
どっ
I'D GET A TON OF HAIR AT ONCE IF CRIM AGREED...
AHHH, AND I'D LOOOVE SOME BLOOD!
I KNOW ANGELS DON'T GET SICK, BUT HOW DOES THAT EVEN WORK?
I WANNA FIND OUT HOW THEIR IMMUNE SYSTEMS WORK! I WANNA PRODUCE A CURE-ALL!

YOU KNOW, I'D EVEN WANT SOME ANGEL SH●T.

WON'T IT BE FULL OF SOME KIND OF WEIRD BACTERIAL FLORA THAT'S EVEN ABLE TO FULLY DIGEST POISON?

OOOH, I WANNA LEARN MORE ABOUT IT! I WANNA RESEARCH IT AND CULTURE IT AND SHOVE IT UP THE ASSES OF ALL KINDS OF SPECIES AND OBSERVE THE EFFECTS...

HAAH.

HAAH.

HAAH.

AH!

OH DEAR, OH DEAR...

I'M JUST LETTING MY DESIRES FLOW OUT OF ME TODAY, AREN'T I...?

JAAAA (SPLIIISH)

FOR NOW, I NEED TO FOCUS ON REPLENISHING MY STOCK OF ANGEL JUICE THAT I USED UP DURING RESEARCH...
...AND CONTENT MYSELF WITH RECOVERING WHATEVER MATERIALS I CAN WHILE CLEANING UP HERE.
IT'LL ALL BE FOR NAUGHT IF CRIM GETS CREEPED OUT BY ME...
I SHOULD ACT RELAXED HERE AND NOT BE TOO GREEDY.
PATA (THWAP)
PATA
IF I DISCOVER HOW TO FIX AN ANGEL'S HALO THROUGH MY RESEARCH...
...I'LL ACCOMPANY THEM STRAIGHT UP TO THE HEAVENS, AND...

SUU (SWOOSH)
...MAYBE I'LL EVEN BE ABLE TO GET MY HANDS ON SOME MATERIALS FROM THE GODS...
MEH HEH HEH. ♥
GO (RUMBLE)
GO
GO
GO

HM?
FOUND ANOTHER HAI—
!?
GUIII (TUUUUUG)
WHAT...?
...A SIGNAL...!!
KU (THP)
KUN (THWIP)
KUN
NO...
KUI (TWING)
THIS IS...
KUI
KU
KUN
UNDERSTAND? UNDERSTAND? PLEASE RESPOND. PLEASE RESPOND.

I DO... BUT...
...WHO ARE YOU?

"I'M AN ANGEL.
"ONE WHOSE HALO ISN'T BROKEN."

HEY, CRIM!
WHERE'S THAT NEXT BOTTLE OF BULL JUICE?
BULL JUICE
IT'S ON ITS WAY!
BULL
I'LL BE RIGHT TH—
HEY.
BFFT!!
NU (BLOOP)
AAA-AGH!
BIKU (TWITCH)
POOOI (TOSS)
AGH!!
GASHAAA (KRAAASH)
GROSS!!
BLEGH!

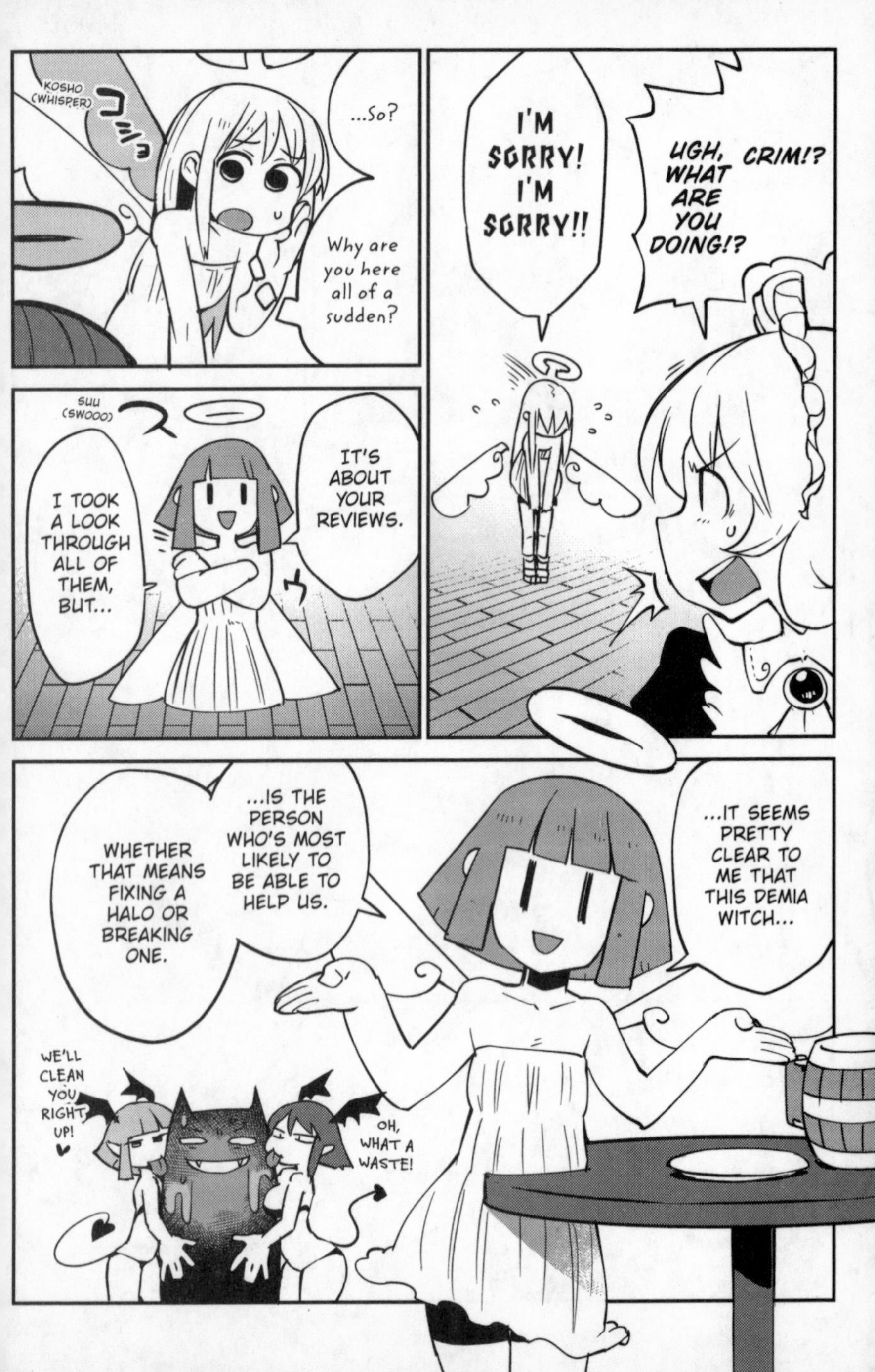
UGH, CRIM!? WHAT ARE YOU DOING!?
I'M SORRY! I'M SORRY!!
...So?
Why are you here all of a sudden?
KOSHO (WHISPER)
IT'S ABOUT YOUR REVIEWS.
I TOOK A LOOK THROUGH ALL OF THEM, BUT...
SUU (SWOOO)
...IT SEEMS PRETTY CLEAR TO ME THAT THIS DEMIA WITCH...
...IS THE PERSON WHO'S MOST LIKELY TO BE ABLE TO HELP US.
WHETHER THAT MEANS FIXING A HALO OR BREAKING ONE.
OH, WHAT A WASTE!
WE'LL CLEAN YOU RIGHT UP!

WELL...I UNDERSTAND YOUR POINT.
BUT EVEN SO, WHAT DO YOU WANT ME TO DO?
IT'S SIMPLE.
YOU NEED TO OFFER HER A SAMPLE...
...OF AN ANGEL'S BODY.
BLOOD, FLESH, IT DOESN'T MATTER.
I COULDN'T BELIEVE IT... AS SOON AS SHE REALIZED I COULD ONLY INTERACT WITH PARTS OF YOU HERE IN THIS WORLD...
...SHE IMMEDIATELY PULVERIZED A STRAND OF YOUR HAIR AND COMBINED IT WITH LUBE.
TORO (BLURP)
SHE LIGHTLY COVERED ONE OF HER EARDRUMS IN A LAYER OF IT, AND...
I SHOULD BE ABLE TO HEAR THE VIBRATIONS OF YOUR VOICE NOW.
GO AHEAD AND TRY SAYING SOMETHING.
HUH...
YOU WERE ABLE TO THINK OF SOMETHING LIKE THAT ON THE SPOT...?
WOW...
THERE REALLY IS SOMETHING I CAN'T SEE IN HERE...

WOW...
...SHE'S ABLE TO DO THAT WITH JUST A STRAND OF MY HAIR...?
SCARY.
GOSHI (SCRUB)
GOSHI
ANYWAY, GIVE HER WHATEVER MATERIALS SHE WANTS.
THEN JUST LEAVE THE REST TO HER UNMATCHED CURIOSITY.
ZUBU (BLURP)
ZUBU
ZUBU
I'LL TELL HER WHAT SHE NEEDS TO KNOW...
...ABOUT US ANGELS.
ZU
ZU (ZZT)
SEE YOU AROUND.
SUU (SWOOO)
......
HMMM...

HEY! CRIM! WHY AREN'T YOU CLEANING!?
TIDY UP ALREADY AND TAKE THIS NEXT ORDER OUT!
KIII (SKREEECH)
ACK...
OKAY!
GASHAA (KRAAASH)
SHUUUU (HISSSS)
WH... WHAT'S WRONG, DEMIA!?
EVERY-THING OKAY?

WHAT'S THE MATTER? WHAT HAPPENED!?
EXHAUSTED FROM THE RESEARCH !?
YOU OUGHT TO TAKE A BREAK BEFORE IT STARTS AFFECTING YOUR HEALTH!
わた WATA
わた WATA (FLUSTER)
IF YOU COLLAPSE HERE, ALL WE'LL BE LEFT WITH IS A MOUNTAIN OF DEBT!
...THE ANGELS HAVE BEEN CAUSING ALL OF THE CHURCH'S SO-CALLED MIRACLES?
ANGELS ARE USUALLY IMPOSSIBLE TO OBSERVE...
...AND THESE INVISIBLE ANGELS ARE EVEN SURVEILLING THE POWERFUL HERE IN THIS WORLD?
ONLY A SELECT FEW ON THE SURFACE ARE ABLE TO DETECT ANGELS.
FORTY-EIGHT INDIVIDUALS ABOVE THE RANK OF ARCHBISHOP OF THE FLASPA CHURCH, INCLUDING HEROES AND GENERALS WHO'VE RECEIVED PERMISSION FROM THE MONK-EMPEROR...
WHAT...? HOW COULD THIS BE?
AND THAT MONK-EMPEROR IS NONE OTHER THAN...

ALL OF THAT WAS SUPER-TOP-SECRET INFORMATION THAT'D EARN YOU AN ON-THE-SPOT EXECUTION IF THEY SO MUCH AS LEARNED THAT YOU LEARNED IT...
...AND THAT ANGEL JUST TOSSED IT OUT THERE LIKE IT WAS NOTHING.
WHAT AN UNBELIEVABLE ANGEL...
THERE'S CLEARLY SOMETHING WRONG WITH THEIR HEAD.
ARE YOU REALLY OKAY?
HEY!!
IT LOOKS LIKE I'VE GOTTEN MYSELF INTO SOMETHING REAL BIG HERE...
...BUT THERE'S NO OPPORTUNITY MORE EXCITING TO ME AS A RESEARCHER EITHER...

ONCE I STARTED LICKING ALL THAT BULL JUICE OFF OF YOU, I STARTED TO WANT SOME OF YOURS AS WELL...! ♥
HEH-HEH-HEH...
C'MON, LET'S HURRY UP AND GO TO YOUR ROOM! ♥
DIDN'T I JUST SAY THAT THIS ISN'T A COUPLES' INN!?
TAKE IT OUTSIDE!!
DOKAA (THWAKK)
IT'S CONSIDERED FREE LOVE AND NOT SUCCU-JOINT ACTIVITIES IF NO MONEY CHANGES HANDS, SO YOU'RE LEGALLY IN THE CLEAR! ♥

ガヤ
GAYA (CHATTER)
ガヤ
GAYA
CHAPTER 38

SINCE I'M ALONE TODAY...
...MAYBE I'LL GO TO A PLACE WITH HUMANS.

HEY THERE, ZEL!

YOU ALONE? DON'T SEE THAT EVERY DAY.
PERFECT.

WE'VE GOT A BRAND-NEW GIRL WHO JUST STARTED WORKING AT OUR STORE.
...WHY DON'T YOU GO AND DO THE HONORS FOR HER?

HUH... FRESH MEAT, HUH?
I LIKE IT. I'M IN!

......!!
GUH...!!
GUH... GU-GU-GU...
GU-GU-GOOD EVENING! MEET TO NICE YOU!
HRAAAGH!
T-TODAY... UM... TODAY...?
LET'S HAVE SOME FUN.
Y-YEAH! THAT! LET'S HAVE LOTS OF FUN TODAY, PLEASE!

YAINO (BLAH)
OH! UM, AND THEN...
...!
YAINO
UMM... HMM?
IS THAT EVERYTHING I NEED TO SAY...?
?
...SHE SURE SEEMS WORKED UP.
YEAH...
WELL... I'LL LEAVE THE REST TO YOU.
I'M. UH. NEW HERE...
!!
HUH? AFTER THAT IS...

SO...
YEP.
SHE PASSES THE FIRST TEST... SHE'S AT LEAST HOLDING MY ARM AS WE HEAD TO THE ROOM.
ZURU (DRAG)
ズル
ZURU
ズル
PAKU (PLOK)
ぱく
PAKU
ぱく
PAKU
ぱく
A-ARE YOU NOT COMING WITH US, MA'AM...?

WHY THE HELL WOULD I?
HURRY UP AND GO.
BUUUH...

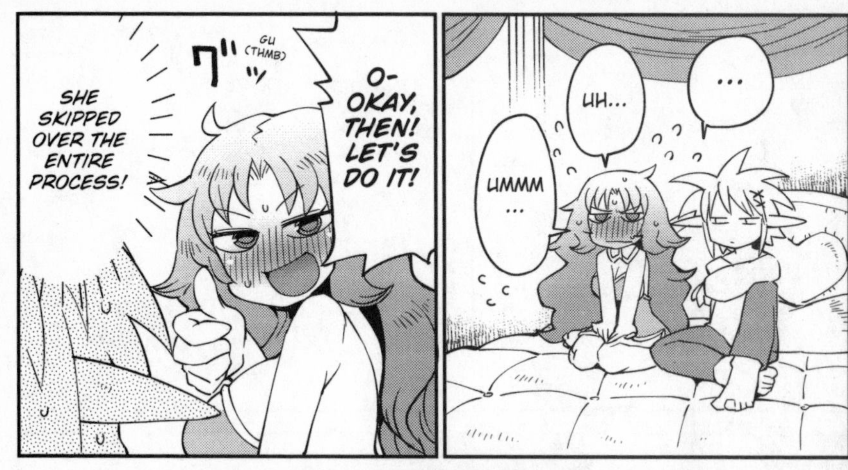
...
UH...
UMMM...
O-OKAY, THEN! LET'S DO IT!
GU (THMB)
SHE SKIPPED OVER THE ENTIRE PROCESS!

HEY, YOU NEED TO CALM DOWN.
WHY DON'T WE CHAT A LITTLE FIRST?
N...NICE WEATHER TODAY, HUH?
HRRK...
GRRK...
WAS IT STILL CLEAR OUT?
THIS IS NO GOOD...

IF YOU'RE WITH SOME-ONE OF YOUR OWN SPECIES...
...THEN MAYBE SMALL TALK ABOUT THE WEATHER IS ALL YOU CAN DO. BUT...
...IF YOU'RE WITH ANOTHER SPECIES, IT MIGHT BE BETTER TO LEAD WITH HOW YOUR SPECIES IS DIFFERENT FROM THEIRS.
...DIFFER-ENCES IN SPECIES?
?

FOR EXAMPLE. YOU'RE A HUMAN, I'M AN ELF.
HOW DO HUMANS VIEW ELVES AS A SPECIES?
UMM...THEY USUALLY LIVE IN FORESTS, ARE GOOD AT MAGIC...
...AND I'M JEALOUS OF THEM BECAUSE THEY'RE ALWAYS YOUNG?
HMMMM...

NOPE! WRONG.
WRONG?
ELVES DO AGE AS THE YEARS PASS.
MAYBE NOT OUR BODIES, BUT OUR SOULS AND OUR MANA DO GET OLDER.

ON THE OTHER HAND, HUMANS HAVE YOUNG SOULS AND MANA UNTIL THEY DIE.
FROM AN ELF'S POINT OF VIEW, YOU HUMANS ARE THE SPECIES THAT STAYS FOREVER YOUNG.

I...I DON'T KNOW IF I REALLY UNDER-STAND...?
YEAH, I GUESS NOT.
I DON'T GET IT WHEN HUMANS SAY THAT ELVES STAY YOUNG EITHER.
HA HA...
• • • •
?
...SO.
FEELING RELAXED NOW?
IN THAT CASE...
...WANNA HEAD TO THE BATH?

BUH... BATH...?
YUH-YUH... YES!!
DOKIIIN (BADOOOMP)
DON'T WORRY! I'M RELAXED NOW!!
LET'S GO! LET'S GO!!
UH, YEAH.
TRY TO BE A LITTLE SEXIER WHEN YOU STRIP.
ZURURUN (FWOOMP)
SHAWAWAWAWA (FSHHHHHHHH)
LET ME WASH YOUR BODY FOR YOU!
SURE.
BUT THAT'S LUBE, YOU KNOW.
HUH!?
BUBYU (SPLURP)
Body Soap
AAAGH!
SORRY I'M SO AWKWARD! I REALLY AM!!
GOSHI (SCRUB)
GOSHI
SURE.
BUT YOU SHOULD GIVE YOUR CUSTOMER A TOWEL BEFORE YOU START USING ONE.
POTA
POTA (DRIP)
AAHH! I'M SORRY!!
GOSHI

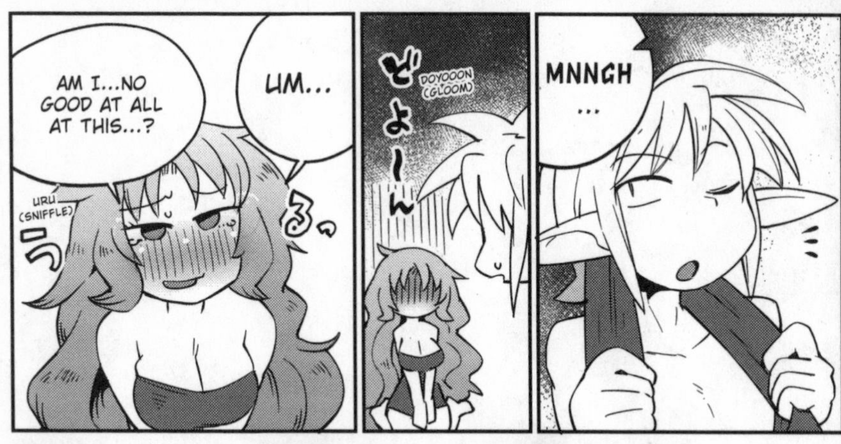

MNNGH ...
DOYOOON (GLOOM)
UM...
AM I...NO GOOD AT ALL AT THIS...?
URU (SNIFFLE)

YOU'RE AWFUL!
WHAT DO YOU WANT ME TO SAY!?
WHAT!!?
GAN (GUH)

AND A GIRL AS BAD AS YOU...
GUI (TUG)
AH!
...DESERVES SOME PUNISHMENT IN BED!
WAI—
HIYAAA!
EEP!

HAAH.

HAAH.

WELL.

HAAAAH♥

HAAAAH♥

I KNOW I SAID ALL THOSE THINGS EARLIER...

THREE MONTHS FROM NOW...
HM?
ONE MORE TIME... PLEASE JUST COME BACK ONE MORE TIME...
...NO, ANYTIME IS OKAY...
I PROMISE I'LL ACE EVERYTHING THEN...
...CUSTOMER SERVICE INCLUDED!
I SEE. GOOD RESPONSE.
HOW COULD I NOT COME BACK AFTER HEARING SOMETHING LIKE THAT?

OH!

HEY, I'M BACK.

GAYA (CHATTER)
GAYA
YE PUBBE

ZEL! WELCOME BACK!
TOTE (BLOOP)
TOTE

WHERE'D YOU GO TODAY?
I WASN'T ON AN ADVENTURE TODAY.

I WENT TO HAVE FUN AT AN AMUSEMENT PARK FOR ADULTS!

AN AMUSEMENT PARK!?

I WANNA GO! I WANNA GO TOO!

IT MIGHT BE A LITTLE TOO SOON FOR YOU, SINCE IT'S FOR ADULTS...

...BUT IN TEN YEARS YOU CAN GO TO THE INCUBUS DISTRICT...

DON'T TEACH IVY WEIRD THINGS LIKE THAT!!

SUKAAAN (THWAKK)

HONESTLY... YOU TOO, IVY. DON'T GET SO FRIENDLY WITH PERVY GUYS LIKE HIM, OKAY?

HIS TYPE'S BAD FOR YOUR UPBRINGING.

BOO-BOO BEGONE!

HEY, WAYBEE! DON'T HIT ME LIKE THAT OUT OF NOWH—
GO (THWAK)
BFFT!!
!?
LIAR! YOU ABSOLUTELY HIT M—
AAH! OWW!
HEY!?
GOSU (KLOK)
GAN (KLANG)
GON (GLONK)
WHY'D YOU HIT ME AGAIN!?
HEY!
?
I DIDN'T DO ANYTHING.
GAN
GAN
GAN
MRR... NNGH...
HOW LONG ARE YOU SLEEPING FOR, ZEL?
THE STORE'S ABOUT TO CLOSE.
KON (THONK)
GON
GOSU
UNNGH...

HM...?
WAIT, WHERE'S WAYBEE...?
WAYBEE?
WHO'S SHE?
OH... MEIDRI.
SO IT WAS ALL A DREAM...
I WANT TO SAY THAT WAYBEE...
...WAS THE WAITRESS BEFORE THE WAITRESS BEFORE THE WAITRESS BEFORE THE WAITRESS BEFORE YOU HERE.
HOW MANY DECADES AGO IS THAT...?
AH!
WAIT, MEIDRI!
DID YOU SAY YOU'RE CLOSING UP NOW!?
THAT'S RIGHT. STORE'S CLOSING.
SO HURRY UP AND LEAVE.
CRAP! MY DATE WITH MISS MITSUE!
BATA (CLATTER)
バタ
BATA
バタ
BATA
バタ
I'LL PAY THE TAB TOMOR-ROW!

HONESTLY.

HE'S LIVED THAT LONG AND STILL ACTS LIKE A KID...

GAYA (CHATTER)

ガヤ

GAYA

ガヤ

YOU KEPT ME WAITING...

...ZEL.

HEY, I'M REAL SORRY ABOUT THAT.
GUESS I FELL ASLEEP AT THE PUB...
TA
タッ
TA (THP)
タッ
TA
タッ
BUT THANKS TO THAT...
...I GOT TO DREAM ABOUT YOU, MISS MITSUE!
ABOUT THE VERY FIRST TIME WE MET...
OH, YOU! HOW EMBARRASSING!
I STILL BLUSH WHEN I THINK BACK TO HOW FLUSTERED I GOT IN THOSE DAYS.
BUT WHAT YOU TAUGHT ME BACK THEN...
...HAS STARTED TO MAKE SENSE TO ME LATELY...
?
...UM...HM? WHAT DID I TELL YOU AGAIN...?
HEH HEH HEH...
THAT WOMEN NEVER LOSE THEIR SHINE! ♥

HOW LONG HAS ZEL BEEN COMING TO YE PUBBE, IVY?
WELL, ZEL'S OLD ADVENTURING PARTNER—FROM BEFORE HE JOINED UP WITH STUNK—GOT MARRIED TO THE PROPRIETRESS HERE AND HAD ME, SO...ALL I CAN REALLY SAY IS THAT HE'S BEEN COMING SINCE BEFORE I WAS BORN...

CHAPTER 39

OOO (WHOOSH)
...STAY QUIET.
KEEP YOUR BODY AS LOW AS POSSIBLE.
AND DO NOT BY ANY MEANS TOUCH EVEN A THREAD...
FUWA (FWOOF)
TSUN (TAP)

PIKUN (TWITCH)

KASA (SCURRY)

TA (THP)

!

GASHI (GRASP)

HYUO (WHOOSH)

CRIM!!!

AAAAGH!

GYUN (SWOOSH)

KASA

AH...

AHH...!

KASA

SHLURP...

SLURP...

...IT'S OVER FOR HIM NOW.

THERE'S NO SAVING HIM.

WE SHOULD FORGET ABOUT HIM AND KEEP GOING.

FAREWELL, CRIM.

WE'LL ALWAYS REMEMBER YOU...

GOSO (CRAWL)

GOSO

OF COURSE...

...THIS IS A PERFECTLY SAFE SUCCU-JOINT.

OOH-LA-LAM

THE ARACHNID NEST

THE ARACHNID NEST.

FIVE MINUTES EARLIER
SIRS...
IS THIS YOUR FIRST TIME AT OUR ESTAB-LISHMENT?
WE ONLY OFFER A 5,000G COURSE.
RECEPTION
PLEASE INSERT PAYMENT
WE OFFER NO OTHER SERVICES.
HUH. FINE WITH ME, BUT...
HOW LONG DO WE GET?
CAN WE PICK A GIRL?
YOU MAY NOT SPECIFY EITHER.
WE CAN'T !?
NO.
FIRST, YOU PAY 5,000G HERE...
...AND THEN YOU ENTER THE STORE...

CLEAR!

THE MONEY YOU PAID SITS IN ITS FARTHEST DEPTHS.

TRY TO MAKE IT THAT FAR TO RECLAIM YOUR GOLD.

OH?

SO THIS PLACE IS TAILOR-MADE FOR THIEVES.

WE'LL SNATCH YOU UP BEFORE YOU MAKE IT TO THE END AND VIOLATE YOU!

LIKE A PROPER ARACHNE WOULD!

...OH, SO THAT'S WHY WE CAN'T PICK A GIRL...

HOLD ON A SECOND. THAT'S GREAT AND ALL, BUT WHAT DO WE GET TO DO WITH THE GIRLS?

HOW'S THE SEXY STUFF WORK?

...WHICH BRINGS US TO NOW.

SHEESH...

THERE ISN'T A SINGLE OPENING.

GETTING THROUGH THIS IS GONNA BE PRETTY HARD...

!?
DA (DASH)
DOKA (THWAK)
STUNK!?
BUCHI (SNAP)
BUCHI
BUCHI

FORGET ABOUT ME!
USE THIS OPENING TO KEEP GOING!
STUUUNK!!
BETO (SPLAP)
WELL, I MEAN...! IF WE WORK OUR ASSES OFF AND MAKE IT THROUGH THIS PLACE...
DOOON (BOOOM)
...ALL THAT'S WAITING FOR US IS THE 5,000G WE JUST PAID, RIGHT!?
I JUST WANT TO HURRY UP AND DO IT!
SO I'M DROPPING OUT HERE!
WELL, YEAH...
TRUE...
SEE YA!
ZURUN (DRAG)

AGH...
STILL, I CAN'T LET MYSELF BE DEFEATED BY A TRAP DUNGEON...
EVEN IF IT IS A SUCCUBUS JOINT, IT'D REFLECT ON MY HONOR...
GAAAH...
I'M MAKING IT TO THE END, ZEL!

UH, SURE.
IN THAT CASE, LET ME HANDLE IT THE NEXT TIME YOU NEED SOMEONE TO ACT AS BAIT...
HAVE YOU LOST INTEREST IN BEATING THIS DUNGEON TOO!?

OH... ANOTHER MESS OF THREADS THAT WE'D NEVER BE ABLE TO PASS THROUGH...
MOSSARI (FWOOF)
もっさりー…
WE CAN'T USE FIRE OR BRING IN WEAPONS, SINCE THAT'D BE AGAINST THE RULES. THIS PLACE IS WAY TOO UNFAIR...

VERY WELL!
LET ME HANDLE THIS!
DADA (DASH)
DON (BOOM)
BUCHI (SNAP)
BUCHI
BUCHI
GIRARI (GLARE)
AH-HA-HA! GOTCHA!
CAPTURED ME AN ELF! ♥
NOW COME TO MY NEST!
I'LL SUCK YOU DRY BACK IN MY...HUH?
OH NOOO!
SHE'S GOING TO RAVISH ME!
SHE'S GOING TO RAVISH ME!
GABA (FWOOMP)

HEH HEH HEH.
SU (SST)
THAT'S A DECOY DOLL THAT MISS DEMIA TAUGHT ME HOW TO MAKE.
ZOKU (SHIVER)
NOW C'MON!
THIS IS FOR PUTTING UP AN IMPOSSIBLY HARD AMOUNT OF SILK!
BIKUN (TWITCH)
NGH! HYA-AH!
TIME FOR YOUR PUNISHMENT!
HAH!
AAAAAAAAAH!
MUGYU (SQUEEEZE)
BIKUN
GO WHILE YOU STILL CAN, KANCHAL!

GAAAH!
AGH...
I WANNA TAKE PART IN THAT PUNISHMENT TOO...
BUT FINE!
DA (DASH)
BA (BAM)
ZUZAAA (SLIIIDE)
!!
ZA (ZSST)
DADA
THERE IT IS!
THE MONEY AT THE END!
G
BAAAN (BAAAM)

GASHIII (GRASP)
ガシーッ
HUUUUP!!
TAAAN (SPROING)
ターンッ
THE ARACHNID NEST

...HUH?

WHERE'S THE SEX?

YORUNO GLOSS REVIEW
THE ARACHNID NEST: THIS GAME BALANCE IS A TANGLED MESS!
HUMAN
THIS TIME AROUND WE WENT TO THE ARACHNID NEST. THERE, YOU GO DEEPER AND DEEPER INTO A BUILDING FULL OF SPIDER NESTS AND GET TIED UP AND RAVAGED BY ONE OF THE GIRLS IF YOU RUN INTO ANY OF THE THREADS. THEY BASICALLY SPIN SILK ALL AROUND YOUR BODY SO THEY CAN SUCK YOU DRY WHILE YOU'RE COMPLETELY DEFENSELESS, SO THIS MIGHT BE A GOOD STORE FOR THOSE INTO BONDAGE. THIS DOES MEAN THAT YOU DON'T EVEN GET TO LAY A SINGLE FINGER ON THEM THE ENTIRE TIME, SO YOU WON'T GET TO BE AGGRESSIVE OR GET ANY HANDFULS OF ANYTHING...I'M NOT A FAN OF BEING SUBMISSIVE TO THIS DEGREE.
STUNK
ELF
ARACHNE WILL SENSE EVEN SLIGHT VIBRATIONS IN THEIR THREADS AND COME TO ATTACK YOU, WHICH MEANS THEY HAVE SHOCKINGLY SENSITIVE BODIES. IF YOU START PLAYING WITH THEM, THEY FEEL IT TO THE POINT THAT THEY LOSE THEIR MINDS AND GO LIMP WHEN THEY COME, WHICH IS WHY IT SEEMS THEIR ENTIRE REPERTOIRE CONSISTS OF FULLY RESTRAINING YOU AND GOING ON THE OFFENSIVE. THE NEST-INVASION SITUATION SEEMS LIKE AN EXCUSE TO SET UP THE FACT THAT THIS IS THE ONLY SERVICE THEY OFFER. BECAUSE OF ALL THIS, WHEN I TOOK THE LEAD WITH ONE OF THEM WHO FELL INTO A LITTLE TRAP THAT I SET UP, IT FELT SO GOOD FOR HER THAT SHE STARTED TO CRY. IT WAS FUN, BUT SHE GOT MAD AT ME AFTERWARD. INCIDENTALLY, THEIR SPIDER HALVES SEEM TO BE MORE SENSITIVE THAN THEIR HUMAN TORSOS.
ZEL
HALFLING
THE NEST-INVASION SITUATION GOT MY THIEF BLOOD GOING AT FIRST, BUT IT WAS SO IMPOSSIBLY HARD THAT IT FEELS LIKE THEY NEVER INTENDED FOR YOU TO FINISH IT IN THE FIRST PLACE. ALSO, BECAUSE ALL THE GIRLS ARE STAKED OUT IN THE BEGINNING AND MIDDLE WHERE THEY'RE MOST LIKELY TO CATCH A CUSTOMER, THE LATTER PART WAS SO ABANDONED THAT IT DIDN'T FEEL LIKE MUCH FUN AT ALL...I BARELY FEEL LIKE IT WAS WORTH COMPLETING...I THINK THERE ARE A LOT OF UNFORTUNATE THINGS ABOUT THIS STORE.
KANCHAL
ANGEL
I GOT KIDNAPPED AS SOON AS IT STARTED, WRAPPED UP, AND THEN SUCKED COMPLETELY DRY... I DON'T EVEN KNOW WHAT HAPPENED...
CRIMVAEL
PUBLISHER: ZEL THE ELF
OPENING SOON!♥ NEW STORE INFORMATION
ELVES
ANOTHER ELF FRO
EVEN GREATER TH
AS OLD AS TIME IT
APPED UP IN THE SOFT
OF WINGED HYBRID
LS LIKE A BABY BIRD!

...WHAT DO I DO NOW?
DO I PAY THEM AGAIN AND GET MYSELF KIDNAPPED ON PURPOSE...?
NO, THAT DOESN'T MAKE SENSE. I DON'T WANT TO DO THAT...
AAAHHH! I CAN'T BELIEVE IT! ♥
YOU BEAT THE ARACHNID NEST, MISTER? ♥
THE DAIRY FARM
WOW! THIS IS THE FIRST TIME I'VE EVER SEEN SOMEONE CLEAR IT! ♥
さっ
ゆ
YUSA (BOING)
チラ...
CHIRA (GLANCE)
G
Fin.

EEK!
AH!
AH!
BIKUN (TWITCH)
NAAAAAAH!
IF YOU TOUCH ME LIKE THAT...!
NO!
AH!
ZOKU (SHIVER)
ZOKU
ZOKU
ZOKU
ZOKU
BIKUN
BIKUN
HFF...
HFF...
...CAN YOU BELIEVE IT? SHE GOT CAPTURED INSTEAD!
WHOA... I THINK I'D GO CRAZY IF SOMEONE TOUCHED ME LIKE THAT...

...HEY, STUNK?
HAVE YOU BEEN ADVENTURING LATELY?
KISHI (KREAK)
HM?
CHAPTER 40
...WHY ARE YOU ASKING ALL OF A SUDDEN?
I'M ABLE TO GET BY ON MY REVIEW ARTICLES ALONE, SO...
WELL...
OH, MAYBE NOT THESE DAYS!
HA HA HA!

UM... SORRY IF THIS OFFENDS YOU.
BUT YOU USED TO ALWAYS HAVE A FIRST-RATE WARRIOR'S BODY, STUNK.
RECENTLY, THOUGH...
...I STARTED TO WONDER IF YOU HAVE A LITTLE EXTRA MEAT ON YOU...
PUYO (JIGGLE)

GAYA (CHATTER)
GAYA
YE PUBBE
...HUH. SO YOU'VE BEEN GETTING IT TOO?
I DID HAVE A CREEPING FEELING, THOUGH.
...WE'VE BEEN LIVING TOO EASY OFF OUR ARTICLES.
GAYA
STILL, GOING BACK OUT TO HUNT MONSTERS FOR DAYS JUST TO EARN SOME MONEY...?
MOGU (MUNCH)
MOGU
MOGU
PORI
PORI
PORI (NIBBLE)
CONSIDERING THAT WE'RE IN A SITUATION WHERE WE'D MAKE MORE JUST FOOLING AROUND WITH GIRLS...
GOKU (GLUG)
GOKU
GOKU
...YEAH, I DON'T FEEL MOTIVATED AT ALL.
HUH! REAAALLY?
SO EVEN YOU GUYS WORRY ABOUT YOUR FIGURES?
MAYBE YOU SHOULD START BY NOT GORGING YOUR-SELVES LIKE THAT.
WE CAN'T DO THAT. IT'D BE EVEN WORSE IF WE LOST MUSCLE.
BEING AN ADVENTURER ISN'T JUST ABOUT BEING SLIM.

どよ〜ん
DOYOOON (GLOOM)

YO! HOW'S IT GOING?

BAN (BOOM)

WHAT'S THE MATTER? FAIL A REQUEST OR SOMETHING?

SEEMS LIKE THEY'RE WORRIED ABOUT THEIR BODIES GETTING DULL.

IF ANYTHING, THEY HAVEN'T TAKEN ENOUGH REQUESTS.

I SEE! YEAH, IT CAN BE A PROBLEM WHEN YOUR SIDE GIG GOES TOO WELL!

ALL RIGHT, THEN LEMME INTRODUCE YOU TO MY FAVORITE TRAINING SPOT!

BI (BTT)

A TRAINING-SPOT!?
WHY SHOULD GUYS LIKE US HAVE TO PAY SOMEONE MONEY JUST TO WORK OUT!?
WE'D BE BETTER OFF ADVENTURING!
THOUGHT YOU MIGHT SAY THAT.
DON'T WORRY. THIS TRAINING SPOT IS A SUCCUBUS JOINT.
NOT BAD.
HEH.
AFTER WORKING UP A SWEAT ALONGSIDE MUSCLE-BOUND SUCCU-GIRLS...
...YOU GO ON TO WORK UP A SWEAT WITH THEM IN BED!
WHAT DO YOU THINK OF MY BODY?♥
WHAT ARE WE DOING!?
LET'S GO, EVERYONE!
LEAD THE WAY, BROOZ!
OH... WELL, HAVE FUN.
THAT DOESN'T SOUND LIKE SOMETHING I CAN DO...
...UGH. JUST WHEN I THOUGHT THEY'D BE GETTING SERIOUS...

LET YOUR FISTS (AND MORE) DO THE TALKING!
BODY LANGUAGE
ZUO (GWOOSH)
URRRGH!!
ONE MORE!!
DOGON (THONK)
RAAAH!!!
HUP!!

BUN (TOSS)

GFFT!

DOSAA (THUD)

IF YOU'RE SOMEONE WITH AVERAGE SKILLS, YOU GOTTA PAY FOR THE TRAINING TOO.

BUT IF YOU'RE TOUGH ENOUGH TO BE A SPARRING PARTNER FOR THE GIRLS HERE, THE TRAINING'S FREE.

SHOULD BE EASY ENOUGH FOR YOU GUYS, RIGHT?

OOH, MR. BROOZ! YOU REALLY ARE SO STRONG! ♥

WE'D LOVE TO BE YOUR PARTNERS LATER TOO! ♥

NOT ONLY THAT, STRONG GUYS ARE POPULAR WITH THE LADIES HERE!

MAKES YOU WANT TO TRAIN HARD, RIGHT!?

UH, YEAH...

THE GIRLS ARE ALL...
...GORIL-LAS HERE!!
I DON'T THINK I CAN DO THIS...
ER, BUT, BROOZ! YOU KNOW...
...I-I'M MORE OF A SWORDSMAN, SO...
UH-HUH.
YEAH, TRUE.
WE NEED TO FOCUS ON SPEED AND AGILITY.
WATA (FLUSTER)
WATA
ZEL! KANCHAL! YOU TOO, RIGHT? YOU DON'T TRAIN FOR BATTLES OF POWER...
I DO LIKE THE GIRLS, THOUGH...
YEAH, I WOULDN'T MIND TAKING THE LEAD WITH MUSCULAR GIRLS LIKE THEM.
OH... THEY'RE OKAY WITH THAT PART...?
LET'S GO FOR ONE MORE ROUND!
YEAH!

...YOU KNOW, WHEN WE WENT TO THAT DWARF SHOP, THESE GUYS DIDN'T CARE ABOUT THEIR BEARDS, BUT I GUESS THEY DON'T DISTINGUISH BETWEEN CUTE, TOUGH GIRLS AND PLAIN GORILLAS EITHER...

NO NEED TO WORRY. THEY'VE GOT FACILITIES...
...THAT ARE JUST RIGHT FOR HALFLINGS AND ELVES TOO.

BUT WHAT ABOUT YOU, STUNK?
I THINK YOU'D BE JUST FINE HERE.

NO... I WOULDN'T WANT TO BUILD UP ANY STRANGE MUSCLES.

IT MIGHT AFFECT MY SWORD SPEED IN A NEGATIVE WAY.

HA HA HA!

I'LL LOOK FOR MY OWN TRAINING PARTNER WHO'S JUST RIGHT FOR ME...

...WELL, IT SEEMS LIKE I'M THE ONLY DISSATISFIED ONE HERE, SO I'LL JUST QUIETLY STEP BACK AND LOOK FOR A GOOD GIRL.

ALL RIGHT, THEN.
WONDER IF THERE'S ANY PROMISING GIRLS HERE...
MMH!
SPOTTED SOME SHREDDED WINGED WOMEN!
OH, YOU!
HEE-HEE!
...NICE!
HEY, GIRLS!
SA (SSST)
HEH.
I WAS HOPING TO DO SOME TRAINING MYSELF.
MIND IF I TAG ALONG WITH WHATEVER YOU'LL BE DOING?

FIRST...
...DROP A SANDBAG THAT WEIGHS A FEW DOZEN KILOS FROM UP HERE...
BASA (FLAP)
GA (THWAK)
GAGO (KRAK)
...THEN GRAB IT WITH YOUR FEET...
GASHI (GRASP)
BASA
BASA
...AND FLY BACK UP!
BASA
DOSA (THUD)
LET'S START WITH TEN SETS!
YOU GOT THIS!
HOW COULD I POSSI-BLY DO THAT!!?
I CAN'T FLY!

AH-HA-HA-HA! YEAH, I KNOW.
YOU JUST TALKED TO US BECAUSE WE'RE CUTE, RIGHT?
SORRY, BUT THIS PLACE IS FOCUSED ON TRAINING FIRST.
THE NAUGHTY STUFF IS LIKE A BONUS, YOU KNOW?
YOU OUGHTTA JUST PICK SOMEONE WHO MATCHES YOUR PROFESSION AND SPECIES HERE.
BUT I WILL TELL YOU THE STORE THAT WE NORMALLY WORK AT.
I'LL BE YOUR PARTNER IF YOU SHOW UP THERE, OKAY?
PIRA (FLAP)
Nest in the Sk
...DAMN IT!
MESSING AROUND WITH ME LIKE THAT...
JUST WAIT UNTIL I GO TO THIS PLACE, UNSHEATHE MY MEAT-BLADE, AND MAKE YOU SING...!
...WAIT! THIS STORE IS HUNDREDS OF KILOMETERS AWAY!
I GUESS THAT'S A HARD-BODIED FLYING SPECIES FOR YOU... THEY TRAVEL SO FAR IT DOESN'T EVEN MAKE SENSE...
TEKU (PLOD)
TEKU

BUON
ブォン
BUON (SWOOSH)
ブォン
HMPH!!
HMPH!!
HERE, THEN...
WARRIORS & SWORDSMEN ONLY
BAN (BAM)
I SEEK YOUR INSTRUCTION!
...I WONDER... IF ANY CUTE GIRLS ARE HERE...
BUON
ブォン
BUON
ブォンッ
HMPH!!
HMPH!!
ガチャ
GACHA (GACHAKK)
ガチャ
GACHA

HRM?
PETA (SPLAP)
PETA
AREN'T YOU ONE OF THEM DIRTY REVIEWERS?
HMM ...?
OH! BOSS!
HEY THERE.
GLAD YOU REMEMBERED ME.
MS. URIGO, MANAGER OF THE BOSS'S HIDEOUT, A FANTASY-SCENARIO SUCCUBUS STORE!!
SO YOU COME HERE TO TRAIN TOO?
EVERY DAY I GOT OFF FROM THAT PLACE.
WHAT KINDA BOSS WOULD I BE IF I DIDN'T STAY IN SHAPE?

JI (STARE)

...?

IT MUST BE FATE THAT WE'VE MET AGAIN HERE! WE OUGHT TO TRAIN TOGETHER!

...I CAN MAKE IT WORK!

ALSO... WOULD YOU BE INTERESTED IN THE PART AFTER THE TRAINING TOO, BOSS!?

ALL THESE YOUNG AMAZONS AND DWARFS AROUND AND YOU STILL PICK ME?
GAH-HA-HA!
GUESS THOSE REVIEWS DON'T LIE. YOU REALLY ARE OBSESSED WITH ELVES!

UH...
...SHE'S AN ELF?
YEAH ...
STUNK MANAGED TO SWALLOW THE WORDS THAT NEARLY CREPT OUT OF HIS THROAT.

VARIOUS WINGED WOMAN EXERCISE ROUTINES
EXER-CISE ONE
DROP A HEAVY SANDBAG FROM A HIGH PLACE AND BRING IT BACK!
MAKE SURE TO KEEP YOUR KNEES AT A NINETY-DEGREE ANGLE! THE EXERCISE WON'T BE AS EFFECTIVE IF YOU STRAIGHTEN YOUR LEGS!
X BAD EXAMPLE
EXER-CISE TWO
KEEP STRUGGLING TO LIFT UP A SANDBAG THAT'S TOO HEAVY FOR YOU TO LIFT!
IT'S OKAY TO USE BOTH ARMS!
EXER-CISE THREE
GRAB A BUDDY AND PLAY AERIAL TUG-OF-WAR WITH A SANDBAG!
HOWEVER, MAKE SURE THE BAG IS LIGHT ENOUGH THAT ONE OF YOU CAN HOLD IT UP WITH ONE LEG!
IT'LL BE DANGEROUS IF ONE OF YOU RUNS OUT OF STRENGTH WHILE IN THE AIR IF IT'S TOO HEAVY!

WHOO-HOOO!
BYUUUN (BWOIIING)
PASHI (SNATCH)
CHIRA (GLANCE)
チラ
CHAPTER 41
BA (THB)
GYUO (GWOOSH)
BA

THOSE TWO ARE AMAZING.
THEY'VE BEEN KEEPING UP THE WHOLE TIME.
THEY REALLY ARE.
THIS IS MY FIRST TIME SEEING A DIFFERENT SPECIES MOVE AS FAST AND AGILELY AS A MONKEY HYBRID.
BA (THB)
HMM...
I WISH THEY'D GO A LITTLE FASTER...
THAT'S ASKING A LOT.
PASHI (SNATCH)
MOST OF THE GIRLS HERE ARE JUST SUCCU-GIRLS WHO LIKE EXERCISE.
HYU (WHOOSH)
IT'S NOT LIKE WE CAN PASS THEM, THOUGH...

プリン
PURIN (JIGGLE)
プリン
PURIN
プリン
PURIN
YEAH... WE WON'T GET TO LOOK AT THOSE ASSES IF WE DO...
EH-HEH-HEH.
HEH-HEH.
OH WELL! GUESS WE GOTTA TAKE IT SLOW.
WAH-HA-HA-HA!
WHEEZE...
WHEEZE...

BUON (BWOOMF)
HUP!!!
BO (BFFT)
TSK!
HYU (WHOOSH)
TAN (THP)
PITA (PTT)
EEK!
HEY, THIS GUY'S SERIOUSLY TOUGH!
A SIMPLE MARTIAL-ARTS-LOVING SUCCU-GIRL ISN'T GONNA BE A MATCH FOR HIM.
WOW! AMAZING!
HE EVEN MADE QUICK WORK OF NIGASHIMA!
WHOA!

YOU MIGHT BE THE STRONGEST MAN I'VE EVER MET!
DO YOU HAVE ANY PLANS AFTER THIS!?
HOW ABOUT SPENDING TIME WITH US!?
OH...
LOOK AT YOU! MISTER POPULAR!
SEEMS LIKE YOU WON'T NEED TO BOTHER WITH LITTLE OLD ME!
NO!
BISHI (POINT)
I ALREADY ASKED FOR YOU, BOSS!
IN FACT, IT HAS TO BE YOU!
UH...?
IN FACT, I WANT IT TO BE YOU!
NO NEED TO WORRY ABOUT IT SO MUCH—
URK...

HUH? WHAT? THAT HUMAN IS GETTING IT ON WITH URIGO?

CAN'T BELIEVE IT...

WHEN'D YOU SEDUCE THAT LITTLE BABY SWALLOW?

GUESS WE CAN'T MAKE LIGHT OF YOU AFTER ALL!

DON'T YOU IDIOTS GET THE WRONG IDEA HERE!!

THAT'S NOT IT!!

OOH, URIGO'S BLUSHING.

WEIRD LOOK ON YOU!

HE'S A HUMAN! A HUMAN!!

THIS GUY'S JUST GOT A TOTAL FETISH FOR ELVES, THAT'S ALL!

GURI (GRIND)

GURI

GURI

WELL, DON'T YOU SEEM TO BE ENJOYING YOURSELVES!!
AH-HA-HA-HA-HA-HA-HA-HA!
EVEN FEMRILLA'S HERE?
...SERI-OUSLY?
STRONG MEN ARE BEAUTI-FUL!!
STRENGTH IS BEAUTY!
KA (THKK)

AND THE THOUGHT OF A STRONG FATHER AND A STRONG MOTHER HAVING A CHILD WHO'S EVEN STRONGER THAN THEIR PARENTS...

AH... NO...I'M GETTING WET JUST IMAGINING IT...!

WHAT IS WRONG WITH THIS WOMAN?

I AM THE AMAZON FEMRILLA.

I AM THE MANAGER OF THIS STORE.

I BELIEVE THAT STRONG MEN MUST DO IT WITH STRONG WOMEN, AND SO THIS STORE WAS BORN!

A PLACE FOR THE STRONG TO COME TOGETHER! A TRUE PLACE OF NATURAL LAW.

DO YOU NOT AGREE!?

STUNK TRICARLCO.

THE GENIUS SWORDSMAN WHO ONCE AT THE TENDER AGE OF TWELVE...

...ENTERED INTO A SWORD-FIGHTING COMPETITION ALONGSIDE ADULTS AND CAME OUT VICTORIOUS.

YOU'RE THAT STRONG?

THAT WAS DECADES AGO...

THAT'S RECENT.

...RIGHT, I GUESS YOU ARE AN ELF...

YOU EVEN REMEMBER WHO WON TOURNAMENTS THAT LONG AGO?

OF COURSE NOT.

THE FACT THAT YOU WERE THE YOUNGEST-EVER WINNER STUCK WITH ME, THAT'S ALL...

NOT TO MENTION THAT I USED THAT ARTICLE AS FODDER THREE TIMES BACK THEN...

HAAH. ♥

HAAH. ♥

EXCUSE ME?

IN ANY CASE, I RECOGNIZE YOUR STRENGTH ALREADY!
WANNA DO IT!?
BA (BAM)
OH!
IF THAT'S WHAT THIS IS ABOUT, I'D GLADLY—
TOKA (THWAK)
OWW!?
WEREN'T YOU JUST GOING ON ABOUT HOW YOU'VE JUST GOTTA BE WITH ME OR SOMETHING?
Y...YES. I'D LIKE TO DO IT WITH YOU, BOSS...
OH NO. THE MANAGER'S GOT A PRETTY NICE FACE, BUT I'M LETTING IT ALL GET AWAY FROM ME...

AH-HA-HA-HA! NO, IT'S FINE!
IT MAKES NO DIFFERENCE WHO COMES BEFORE ME! BED THEM ALL, IN FACT!
MONOPOLIZING THE SEED OF A STRONG MAN IS BUT A WASTE OF A COLOSSAL RESOURCE!
HA HA HA

IF MONEY IS THE PROBLEM, I'LL GIVE YOU AS BIG A DISCOUNT AS THE LAW WILL ALLOW!
DON'T HOLD BACK, TAKE THEM ALL! SUCH IS THE DUTY OF STRONG MEN!
UGH...
NO THANKS.....

!?
GA (SNATCH)

PHAH.
GUI (TUG)
SORRY, FEMRILLA.
BUT I'M AWFULLY POSSESSIVE, YOU KNOW?
HE'S ALL MINE, AT LEAST FOR TODAY.
SEE YA!
HEEEY !!
HEY! NO FAIR, URIGO!!
HYAAH!
STOP HOGGING HIM!
LET ME DO HIM TOO!

WH...WHY WERE YOU THAT DEAD SET ON GETTING AWAY FROM THEM?

YOU'RE NOT REALLY... FEELING POSSESSIVE ABOUT ME, ARE YOU?

...IT'S BECAUSE YOU'RE TOO STRONG!

IT'D BE FINE IF YOU WERE JUST AN AVERAGE ADVENTURER WHO'S CONFIDENT IN THEIR SKILLS...

...BUT IT'S A DIFFERENT STORY IF YOU'VE GOT REAL SKILL ON A LEVEL THAT MAKES FEMRILLA OBSESSED WITH YOU.

THE OBSESSION THAT AMAZONS LIKE HER HAVE WITH STRONG MEN...

...ISN'T SOMETHING TO BE TAKEN LIGHTLY.

I DARE YOU TO SLEEP WITH HER ONCE...
I BET SHE'D END UP FORCING HER WAY INTO YOUR HOME AND YOUR WORK EVERY DAY TO COURT YOU...
TAKE ME, MR. STUNK!

THEN AGAIN, IF YOU'RE PREPARED TO HAVE FOUR OR FIVE AMAZONS...
...FORCING THEMSELVES ONTO YOU AS YOUR NEW WIVES, I WON'T STOP YOU.
NO... I'LL PASS...
RIGHT?
BASA (FWWP)
... MORE THAN ANYTHING, I WOULDN'T WANT TO SLEEP WITH ANY OF THOSE GIRLS OTHER THAN THE MANAGER...
THEN AGAIN, THEY'RE TOLERANT ABOUT THEIR MEN SLEEPING AROUND. IN FACT, THEY OPENLY ENCOURAGE IT!
HA HA HA!
SO WHO KNOWS, AN AMAZON MIGHT MAKE A GOOD WIFE FOR A GUY OBSESSED WITH SUCCUBUS JOINTS LIKE YOU! HA!
...YEAH.
ANYWAY, FORGET ALL THAT. I WANT TO DO IT WITH YOU RIGHT NOW.
HUH?
...YEAH, ALL RIGHT. FINE...
BODY LANGUAGE
WE CAN'T REALLY USE THIS STORE AT THE MOMENT, SO WHY DON'T YOU COME OVER TO MINE...?

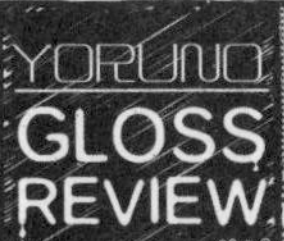

HARD BODIES VS HARD-ONS!

STUNK

6

THIS TIME WE WENT TO AN UNUSUAL SPOT, A TRAINING-CENTER-CUM-SUCCUBUS-JOINT! THE GIRLS WHO WORK THERE ARE ALLOWED TO USE THE FACILITIES FOR FREE AND ARE WORKING OUT HARD. CUSTOMERS ARE ALLOWED TO USE THE TRAINING FACILITIES FOR FREE AS WELL IF THEY'RE STRONG. AFTER YOU EXERCISE TOGETHER WITH A GIRL, IT'S TIME TO HAVE A FIELD DAY WITH HER IN BED TO CAP IT ALL OFF. IT SEEMS THE AMAZON MANAGER CREATED THE STORE IN ORDER TO FISH FOR STRONG MEN, SO THE PRICE IS CHEAP, SINCE PROFITABILITY ISN'T ONE OF HER CONCERNS. THE ONLY PROBLEM IS THAT ONLY SERIOUSLY MUSCULAR SUCCU-GIRLS GO HERE, SO NOT MANY WERE MY TYPE. THE CUTE WINGED WOMEN THERE WERE INVOLVED IN A TRAINING REGIMEN SO DIFFERENT FROM MY OWN THAT THEY WOULDN'T GIVE ME THE TIME OF DAY, WHICH MADE ME FEEL LIKE IT'S A BIT DIFFICULT TO PICK THE RIGHT GIRL HERE. ...ALSO, SINCE THIS IS A STORE BUILT BY AN AMAZON IN ORDER TO FIND STRONG MEN, AMAZONS ARE GOING TO FOLLOW YOU AROUND EVEN OUTSIDE THE STORE IF YOU'RE SEEN AS TOO STRONG, SO BE CAREFUL.

ELF

ZEL

8

A TRAINING FACILITY YOU'RE ABLE TO USE FOR FREE IF YOU'RE STRONG ENOUGH. YOU CAN PROBABLY GET IN FOR FREE IF YOU'RE TOUGH ENOUGH TO HUNT B-RANK BEASTS. THE PROBLEM, THOUGH, IS THAT ADVENTURERS AT THAT LEVEL MIGHT FIND THESE SUCCU-GIRLS WHO JUST LIKE TO WORK OUT LACKING AS TRAINING PARTNERS...THOUGH YOU DO GET TO WORK OUT FOR A LONG TIME WHILE LOOKING AT GIRLS, SO IT'S EASIER TO STAY MOTIVATED THAN IF YOU WERE SURROUNDED BY SCRUFFY DUDES. THE WAY YOU GET TO WORK UP A SWEAT TOGETHER WITH A GIRL, GET FRIENDLY WITH HER, AND THEN GET TO REALLY KNOW HER GETS BOTH SIDES PRETTY EXCITED. IT'S A HOT SITUATION, AND I THINK I LIKE IT.

KANCHAL

8

EVEN THOUGH THIS STORE IS SUPPOSED TO BE OPEN TO SUCCU-GIRLS, IT SEEMS THEY HAVE TO BE AT LEAST SOMEWHAT FIT TO USE IT, MEANING THAT ALL THE GIRLS HERE ARE BUFF. IT MIGHT BE THE PERFECT STORE IF YOU'RE INTO MUSCULAR GIRLS. I GUESS I LIKE THEM ENOUGH. THE PRICE IS SUPER CHEAP TOO.

IT'S ONLY CHEAP IF YOU'RE STRONG, THOUGH. IF YOU GO AS A REGULAR AMATEUR, THE BILL IS GOING TO BE HIGH. THE FACILITIES THEY OFFER ARE ALSO ALL SO INTENSE THAT AMATEURS WON'T BE ABLE TO USE THEM, SO I WOULDN'T RECOMMEND GOING IF THAT APPLIES TO YOU.

BROOZ

10

FIGHT WITH STRONG GIRLS, WORK UP A SWEAT, AND THEN DO IT WITH THEM AT THE END! THIS IS NOTHING SHORT OF THE PERFECT TRAINING FACILITY, PACKED FULL OF EVERYTHING A FIGHTING HYBRID DREAMS OF. NOT ONLY IS IT CHEAP, THEY HAVE AN AMAZING LINEUP OF EQUIPMENT. IT'S EVEN LOADED WITH GIRLS WHO LIKE STRONG GUYS. THIS PLACE IS MY GO-TO.

THE ONE THING THAT WOULD MAKE IT ABSOLUTELY PERFECT IS IF THERE WERE GIRLS OTHER THAN THE MANAGER THERE WHO WERE STRONG ENOUGH TO PUT UP A FIGHT, BUT I REALIZE THAT'S ASKING FOR TOO MUCH.

PUBLISHER:
ZEL
THE ELF

OPENING SOON!♥
NEW STORE INFORMATION

MAGES — LOADED WITH MANA, THEY EACH HAVE THEIR OWN SPECIAL "MAGIC TRICKS." ASK AT THE FRONT DESK.

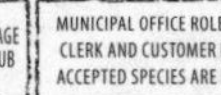

IMAGE CLUB — MUNICIPAL OFFICE ROLE-PL CLERK AND CUSTOMER RO ACCEPTED SPECIES ARE F

GACHA (GACHIK)
ガチャ…
OH. WELCOME HOME, DARLING.
KURU (TURN)
くる
I'LL GET DINNER READY IN JUST A SECOND, OKAY?
"WELCOME HOME"...?
THIS ISN'T YOUR HOME...
HA-HA! YOU SAY THAT...
...BUT YOU ALWAYS LET ME IN ANYWAY. THAT'S WHY I LOVE YOU SO MUCH, DARLING! ♥
YOU KNOW WHAT HAPPENED TODAY...?
ZORO (CREEP)
ゾロ
I FOUND SOMEONE JUST AS STRONG...OR MAYBE EVEN STRONGER THAN YOU.
ZORO
ゾロ
BUT HE BLEW US OFF WHEN AN ELF SNATCHED HIM AWAY!
ZORO
ゾロ

IT MADE ALL OUR HEARTS ACHE SO MUCH...
...AND THAT'S WHY WE SHOWED UP! ♥
WON'T YOU COMFORT US, DARLING? ♥
...NOW THAT I THINK ABOUT IT, I GUESS I FORGOT TO TELL THE OTHER GUYS THAT THE AMAZONS ARE GOING TO FOLLOW YOU AROUND IF YOU SHOW THEM YOU'RE TOO STRONG...
WELL... IT SEEMS LIKE THEY MANAGED TO AVOID IT. I GUESS IT'S FINE...

WHERE DO I NORMALLY WORK? A STORE CALLED "ALPHA OF MONKEY MOUNTAIN." IT'S A STORE THAT ONLY OFFERS ONE THING, A COURSE WHERE YOU RENT OUT A MONKEY HYBRID SUCCU-GIRL HAREM FOR A FULL DAY TO DO WHATEVER YOU WANT WITH THEM!

...WELL, YES. IT IS INCREDIBLY EXPENSIVE. BUT IF YOU'RE THE KIND OF GUY WHO CAN AFFORD IT, WE EVEN START THINKING OF YOU AS AN ALPHA AND IT GETS ALL THE GIRLS SUPER EXCITED.

ZAZAZAZA (ZSSSHHH)
OKAY ...
LET'S GO!
CHAPTER 42
OOOO (WHOOSH)
TO THE BALD EAGLE WINGED WOMAN SPECIALTY STORE—
NEST IN THE SKIES...!
WHERE'S CRIM?
I LEFT HIM BEHIND.
TO BE FRANK, HE WON'T BE ABLE TO KEEP UP HERE...

ガヤ
GAYA (CHATTER)
...HM?
ガヤ
GAYA
STUNK AND THE GANG AREN'T HERE TODAY EITHER?
ガヤ
GAYA

HEY, CRIM?
YES?
DO YOU KNOW WHERE THEY WENT?

THEY SAID THEY WERE GOING ON AN EXPEDITION OUT TO A BIRD OF PREY ***WINGED WOMAN*** STORE.
OH...
OH. I SEE.
I SHOULDN'T HAVE EVEN ASKED.
UGH.
SO?
WHY ARE YOU TAKING A BREAK ***THIS TIME***?
ERR...

W-WELL, IT SEEMS AT THAT STORE YOU HAVE TO CLIMB STRAIGHT UP A TREE...
...THAT'S A FEW HUNDRED METERS TALL...
YOJI (INCH) よじ
YOJI よじ
HUH?

MOO
OOO!
YOU SHOULDN'T, CRIM. THIS IS FOR YOUR OWN GOOD...
THOSE GIRLS ARE STRONG ENOUGH TO FLY AROUND WITH A COW IN THEIR TALONS...!
IF YOU'RE A SPECIES THAT CAN FLY...
...YOU HAVE TO BEAT SOMEONE FROM THE STORE IN TUG-OF-WAR...
VS
HA-HA...
Y-YEAH...
......
SO IN OTHER WORDS, THEY ARE DOING A CRAWL OF STORES WHERE THEY CAN WORK OUT?
WELL, AT LEAST THAT MEANS THEY CAN'T DRAG YOU AROUND WITH THEM.
YE PUBBE

SUU (SWOOP)
BAN (BAM)
GU (GRIP)
HOLD UP, CRIM.
BAAAAN (BAAAM)
YOU'RE GONNA HEAD TO THE SUCCUBUS DISTRICT, RIGHT?
WE'RE TAGGING ALONG!

LULU!
NAL-GAMI!
SAM-TAHN!
YOU HAVEN'T BEEN ABLE TO TAG ALONG WITH STUNK AND THEM LATELY, SINCE THEY KEEP GOING TO STORES THAT REQUIRE ENDURANCE, RIGHT?
THAT'S WHERE WE THOUGHT WE'D STEP IN.
EVERY-ONE...!
WE WANT IN ON THIS WONDERFUL CONTRACT OF YOURS WHERE YOU GET TO HAVE FUN AND MAKE MONEY ON TOP.
THAT'S RIGHT.
AND WELL, WE WANT MONEY FROM REVIEWS TOO.
OH.
OKAY...

...SO.
IS THERE ANYWHERE IN PARTICULAR YOU WANTED TO VISIT?

ANYWHERE IN PARTICULAR...? NOT REALLY.

...YEAH, MAYBE A PLACE WITH PLAIN-COLORED GIRLS...

THERE?

AND ONES WHO AREN'T TOO BIG...

I'D LIKE A GIRL WHO COILS HERSELF AROUND ME, OR MAYBE ONE WHO LOOKS EASY TO SWALLOW.

OR MAYBE THERE?

OH, AND GIRLS WHO LAY EGGS WOULD BE NICE...

HOW ABOUT ...?

IT'S NOT THAT I HAVE ANYTHING SPECIFIC IN MIND...

...SOMETHING LIKE...?

...BUT I WOULD LIKE A STORE WITH A CLEAR-CUT SYSTEM AND DIRECTION...

YOU KNOW, YOU HAVEN'T BEEN INVITING NALGAMI OR LULU ALONG MUCH LATELY.
IS THERE A REASON FOR THAT?
EH...
THEIR TASTES...OR RATHER, THE CHARACTERISTICS OF THEIR SPECIES, ARE A LITTLE TOO MUCH FOR US...
BUT TO PUT IT BLUNTLY...
...THEY'RE A PAIN IN THE ASS.
UUUGH...
OH... SO THIS IS IT.
NOW I SEE EXACTLY WHAT THEY MEANT BY THAT...
WHY ARE YOU SO OBSESSED WITH PLAIN GIRLS?
DON'T BRIGHT COLORS LOOK MASCULINE TO YOU?
...NOT AT ALL.
IS IT BECAUSE MALE BUTTERFLIES TEND TO BE COLORFUL...?
T-TO BE HONEST, I CAN'T THINK OF ANYWHERE LIKE THAT...
WHY DON'T WE LOOK AT THE GIRLS ON THE STREET AND DECIDE ON A STORE WE ALL LIKE THAT WAY...?

WELCOME!♥
WHAT ABOUT MINO-GIRLS!?
THEY'D CRUSH ME...
I'M NOT THAT INTO BOOBS...
YOU'VE ALREADY REVIEWED THEM. YOU CAN'T MAKE THAT AN ARTICLE.
COW HYBRIDS
FAIRIES
CAT HYBRIDS
ARACHNE
NOT A GOOD FIT...
AND I MEAN THAT IN MUL-TIPLE WAYS...
I'M NOT GREAT WITH CAT HYBRIDS.
IT'S NOT AS BAD AS BIRDS OF PREY OR MONGOOSES, BUT STILL...
PURU (SHIVER)
PURU
NO WAY, NO WAY, NO WAY!!
PHYSIO-LOGICALLY IMPOSSI-BLE!!
ZUZAZA (ZSSST)

WE JUST CAN'T COME TO AN AGREEMENT...
HM?
SAMTAHN, ARE YOU OKAY WITH ANYWHERE ...
...THAT'S NOT THE DAIRY FARM?
...YEAH.
I'M JUST HERE AS PART OF THE REVIEW CONTRACT THAT YOU GUYS CREATED.
HEH...
I'LL GO ALONG WITH ANYTHING SO LONG AS IT'S NOT A STORE YOU'VE ALREADY REVIEWED.
HMM...
HIS SPECIES REALLY IS OBSESSED WITH CON-TRACTS...
NOT THAT IT'S ANNOYING, THOUGH.

DOTA (THMP)

WHOA!

... OH...

HEH-HEH... WANNA COME TO MY PLACE?

BATA (WHMP)

LET'S PLAY, MISTER! MEE-YOW!

MY TAIL ISN'T A TOY!!

YEEEEEK!!

EVEN SO, SOMETIMES THE SUCCU-GIRLS GET SUPER EXCITED OVER CUSTOMERS WHO ARE SPECIES THAT CAN'T STAND THEM...

DIFFERENCES IN TASTE BETWEEN SPECIES IS SUCH A TOUGH PROBLEM...

SAMTAHN SAYS HE'LL GO ALONG WITH WHATEVER THEY SAY, BUT THAT ALSO MEANS HE WON'T MAKE A CHOICE ON HIS OWN...

HRMM...
WHAT SHOULD I DO...?
HEY, YOU, THE ANGEL OVER THERE!
WANT TO HAVE A GOOD TIME WITH ME?
UMM...

...YOU KNOW, WHATEVER'S FINE!

OH, YEAH!

SURE, IF MY FRIENDS ARE OKAY WITH IT!

GAVE UP!

NAL-GAMI!

LULU!

WHAT DO YOU THINK ABOUT THIS STORE?

CHAPUN (SPLURCH)

A SLIME?
NO...
HER BODY'S TOO WATERY.
THAT MUST BE AN UNDINE.
OKAY, FINE WITH ME! LET'S GO!
I CAN'T REALLY IMAGINE WHAT IT'LL BE LIKE, BUT OKAY, I GUESS...
WHAAAT? WAIT UP!
MR. WRIGGLY ...

WE WENT TO AN UNDINE STORE!♪

ANGEL

WE WENT TO A STORE WITH WATER SPIRITS KNOWN AS UNDINES. THEIR SPECIAL POINT IS THAT THEIR BODIES ARE MADE UP ALMOST ENTIRELY OF HOLY WATER, AND THAT HOLY ELEMENT FELT EXTREMELY COMFORTABLE TO ME. UNLIKE SLIMES, THEY FEEL ALMOST IDENTICAL TO WATER WHEN YOU TOUCH THEM. WHILE THERE'S JUST ABOUT ZERO STIMULATION WHEN YOU PUT IT INSIDE, HER QUICK AND POWERFUL SUCTION MADE FINISHING NO PROBLEM AT ALL... WHAT EXACTLY IS THIS FEELING? COMING THANKS TO THE SENSATION OF RUNNING WATER IS...SO DIFFERENT FROM NORMAL THAT I DON'T KNOW HOW TO EXPLAIN IT...

LAMIA

I KNOW THEY SAY THEIR BODIES ARE MADE OF HOLY WATER AND THAT CRIM WAS CRAZY ABOUT THIS PLACE, BUT I DON'T GET IT AT ALL. EVEN IF I COILED MYSELF AROUND MY GIRL, SHE DIDN'T HAVE A BODY TO CONSTRICT, SO IT JUST FELT LIKE NOTHING TO ME. BUT THE WAY SHE WAS LIKE A HOLE THAT SUCKED ME IN WAS SO NEW! IT KIND OF FEELS LIKE STICKING YOUR YOU-KNOW-WHAT INTO A DRAIN AND GETTING OFF USING THE WATER PRESSURE, BUT IT WAS EVEN BETTER, SINCE THE SUCTION HAD A MIND OF ITS OWN. IN ANY CASE, IT'S A FRESH NEW FORM OF STIMULATION THAT'S WORTH TRYING AT LEAST ONCE. WORTH GOING IF YOU LIKE NEW EXPERIENCES.

FAIRY

LULU

I THOUGHT IT'D BE THE SAME AS SLEEPING WITH A SLIME GIRL... BUT I NEVER IMAGINED IT WOULD BE THIS DIFFERENT. TOUCHING HER FELT EXACTLY LIKE WATER, SO SUCTION IS THE ONLY WAY SHE CAN STIMULATE YOU. UPSTAIRS, DOWNSTAIRS, EITHER MOUTH SUCKS YOU THE SAME WAY. WHAT'S NICE FOR SMALL FAIRIES IS THAT YOUR SIZE AND THE SIZE OF HER HOLE DON'T REALLY MATTER. OF COURSE, THAT GOES FOR SLIMES AS WELL, PLUS YOU CAN CHOOSE A COLOR WITH THEM. UNDINES ARE ALL TRANSPARENT, SO I MIGHT LIKE SLIME GIRLS MORE OVERALL...IT DOESN'T SEEM LIKE ANY GRAY UNDINES EXIST...HER BODY WAS HOLY WATER, I GUESS? I DON'T REALLY KNOW.

DEVIL

I WAS STRICKEN BY AN INTENSE FEELING OF DISPLEASURE DUE TO HER HOLY-ELEMENT BODY MADE OF HOLY WATER...STILL, I NEEDED TO SLEEP WITH HER IN ORDER TO WRITE THIS REVIEW, AND SO I PERSISTED. AS SOON AS MY BODY ENTERED INTO HER HOLY WATER FIGURE, THOUGH...WELL, I CAN'T REMEMBER THE REST. AM I UNABLE TO REMEMBER...OR DID I BLACK OUT...?

Publisher: Crimvael

IF YOU CAN'T DO IT, JUST SAY YOU CAN'T!

BUT... ONCE THE THREE OF YOU MADE UP YOUR MINDS, THE CONTRACT STATES—

DON'T WORRY ABOUT THAT. IF YOU CAN'T DO SOMETHING, JUST TELL US!

WHEN YOU TOUCH ME... YOUR HOLY ELEMENT DEALS DAMAGE TO ME AS WELL...

URK...

AH... S-SORRY... I'M TAKING DARK-ELEMENT DAMAGE FROM YOU TOO...

THE NIGHT WAS A MESS FROM START TO FINISH, AND THE FOUR CAME AWAY REALIZING THAT THEY NEEDED STUNK AND THE OTHERS AROUND AFTER ALL.

TO BE CONTINUED

Miss Demia's INTERSPECIES LOVE LECTURES!

HEY THERE, EVERYONE! ARE YOU FAMILIAR WITH THE SUSPENSION BRIDGE EFFECT?

THAT'S THE PHENOMENON WHERE THEY SAY IT'S EASIER FOR PEOPLE TO FALL IN LOVE WHILE ON TOP OF A SUSPENSION BRIDGE BECAUSE WHEN THE BRIDGE GETS THEIR HEART RACING, THEY MISTAKE IT FOR THEIR HEART RACING DUE TO LOVE!

SIMILARLY, THERE'S SOMETHING KNOWN AS THE PREDATOR EFFECT AMONG MIXED PAIRS OF SPECIES! PREDATORS CONFUSE THE EXCITEMENT OF WANTING TO EAT OR ATTACK THEIR PREY WITH SEXUAL OR ROMANTIC FEELINGS.

THIS MAY SEEM LIKE A ONE-SIDED PHENOMENON AT FIRST, BUT BECAUSE THEIR PREY GETS A RACING HEART OF THEIR OWN DUE TO THE SUSPENSION BRIDGE EFFECT, IT SEEMS LIKE THERE ARE A GOOD NUMBER OF CASES WHERE THIS LEADS TO COUPLES BEING FORMED!

THEY DON'T LAST LONG, THOUGH.

END-OF-VOLUME BONUS MANGA

AHH! YOU REALLY CAME BACK!

I'M SO HAPPY! HOW LONG HAS IT BEEN, HALF A YEAR?

NOW I'LL BE SURE TO REALLY SHOW YOU A GOOD TIME!

ぱぁっ

PAAA (SHIIINE)

HUMANS REALLY ARE SO QUICK TO ADAPT. JUST A FEW MONTHS, AND SHE'S GROWN TO THE POINT WHERE SHE'S A PROPER SUCCU-GIRL.

I'M LOOKING FORWARD TO IT!

TEN YEARS LATER

GISHI (KREAK)

HEH-HEH... WELCOME, ZEL.

LET'S HAVE A LOT OF FUN TODAY, OKAY...?

O... OKAY... ...MISS MITSUE ...
...AND NOW IT HASN'T EVEN BEEN A DECADE, BUT SHE'S ALREADY BECOME SUCH A VETERAN THAT I'M THE ONE BEING BOWLED OVER BY HER...
THIS IS THE KIND OF DEFYING OF EXPECTATIONS THAT MAKES HUMANS SO GREAT.
THEN IN ANOTHER TWENTY YEARS OR SO, SHE MIGHT GO BACK TO BEING A CUTE GIRL WHO WANTS TO BE SPOILED...WHICH IS GREAT TOO...!

HMMM?
THAT'S STRANGE...
?
WHAT'S WRONG, MANAGER?
NO MATTER HOW MANY TIMES I COUNT TODAY'S SALES, WE'RE MISSING FOUR CUSTOMERS' WORTH...
OH.
THERE WAS THAT FOUR-PERSON GROUP THAT COMPLETED THE STORE TODAY, REMEMBER?
ISN'T IT THEIRS?
I NEVER KNEW!!
IT'S POSSIBLE TO BEAT THIS PLACE!?
...WHAT ARE YOU TALKING ABOUT?
...?

I GOTTA SAY, THIS PLACE IS HUGE...
WELL, IT USES A CAVE THAT'S BEING DUG OUT FOR GEM MINING.
IT SHOULD STILL BE GETTING BIGGER.

WHAT ARE HARD-BODIED HARD LABORERS!?

A FORM OF PUNISHMENT OFTEN IMPOSED ON STARVING BOYS WITH NO MONEY OR PLACE TO GO WHO ARE FORCED TO STEAL FOOD IN ORDER TO LIVE!

IN EXCHANGE FOR ALL THE FOOD THEY CAN EAT, THEY'RE MADE TO WORK IN THE MINES UNTIL THEY'RE MUSCLE-BOUND!

AFTER THEY ARE STRONG ENOUGH TO BE FREED, THEY'RE REHABILITATED BY BECOMING ADVENTURERS OR PHYSICAL LABORERS!

INCIDENTALLY, I HEAR THAT EACH NIGHT, THE YOUNGER HARD-BODIED HARD LABORERS GET VISITED BY BOY-LOVING HARD-BODIED SUCCUBI, WHO MAKE THE BOYS GET HARD-BODIED DOWN BELOW...
WHAT A DARK SIDE OF OUR SOCIETY...
THAT DARKNESS SOUNDS AWFULLY PINK TO ME...

GABA (WHHMP)
GA (GRAB)
HM? AREN'T YOU THAT HUMAN FROM BEFORE?
SERIOUSLY?
YOU REALLY CAME ALL THIS WAY...
HOOH... HAAH ... WHERE IS THE OTHER GIRL?
ZEI (WHEEZE)
ZEI
ZEI
TOWA?
SHE'S ON TOP OF THE TREE BEHIND YOU.

OH, SO IT'S TOWA YOU WANTED?
TCH.
WELL, YOU DID MANAGE TO CLIMB UP HERE.
WANT ME TO TAKE YOU OVER TO HER TREE?

NO, IT'S FINE! I'LL SLEEP WITH YOU THIS TIME!
BISHI (POINT)
HUH?
UH... OKAY... REALLY?
BUT AFTER I DO, I PROMISE YOU I'M CLIMBING UP THE OTHER TREE AND SLEEPING WITH HER TOO!!
I'M GONNA MAKE HER TWEET!
......
YOU'RE REALLY SOMETHING...

HAAAH...

HAAAH...

BY THE WAY. THEY DIDN'T TWEET...

KREE...KREEEK!

PWEEEK!

...SO MUCH AS THEY SOUNDED LIKE THIS.

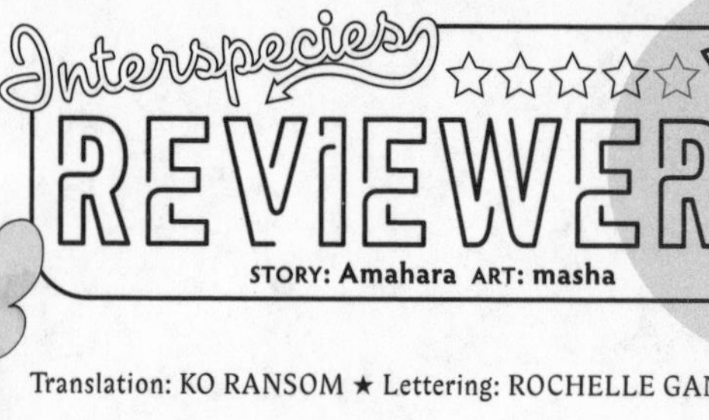

Translation: KO RANSOM ★ Lettering: ROCHELLE GANCIO

Yen Press
150 West 30th Street, 19th Floor
New York, NY 10001

Visit us at yenpress.com ★facebook.com/yenpress ★twitter.com/yenpress
★yenpress.tumblr.com ★instagram.com/yenpress

First Yen Press Edition: June 2021

Library of Congress Control Number: 2018950178

ISBNs: 978-1-9753-2427-8 (paperback)
978-1-9753-2428-5 (ebook)

10 9 8 7 6 5 4 3 2 1

WOR

Printed in the United States of America